TANDEM

KV-513-395

Puzzling You Again

A brain-teasing feast from start to finish,
PUZZLING YOU AGAIN will amuse and
intrigue, frustrate and delight all those
who love to wrestle with challenging puzzles.

The fourth collection of Jonathan Always
puzzles to appear in book form in Tandem,
this book will be eagerly welcomed by
the author's old devotees, and will undoubtedly
gain for him many new ones.

Puzzling You Again

Jonathan Always

TANDEM
14 Gloucester Road, London SW7

First published in Great Britain by
Universal-Tandem Publishing Co. Ltd. 1969

Made and printed in Great Britain by
The Garden City Press Ltd., Letchworth, Herts.

DEDICATED

to

CAROLINE HUTCHISON

and

JANE MOYNIHAN

neither of whom, I am thankful to
say, had an opportunity to hinder
me in the preparation of this book.

P.S. *But I greatly miss both of them.*

CONTENTS

INTRODUCTION

This is my fourth book of puzzles. So if you should think that I cannot stop writing these books, my excuse is that you keep on asking for them. And if you already know a few of the puzzles here (or in any of my earlier books) my excuse for this is that a great many people, both young and old, have never before come across even the oldest puzzles.

Take, for example, a problem I imagine to be at least as old as myself. I nearly said as old as the hills.

A man is looking at the photograph of a certain individual. Then he says:

'Brothers and sisters have I none,
But that man's father is my father's son.'

Whose photograph was it?

The answer is, of course, that he was looking at a photograph of his son.

I asked eight grown-ups that one, and three of them had never heard it before. Of the remaining five, two of them gave me the *wrong* answer!

Most of the puzzles in this book, however, will be entirely new to you; and some of the old ones are presented in a new form.

In conclusion, thank you for permitting me to puzzle you again.

JONATHAN ALWAYS

PUZZLES

AND

PROBLEMS

INITIALLY

1. I always think it is a good idea to begin something at the beginning. Do you not agree?

Well, the word 'initially' means 'at the beginning', so I suggest that we begin this book with a puzzle concerning initials.

What does P.C. stand for? Also, what does it mean if printed in small letters, thus: p.c.? There are several answers.

INITIALLY AGAIN

2. What letter in the alphabet is the first letter of the greatest number of English words? And the smallest number?

MOROCCAN MATHEMATICS

3. More than a thousand years ago, according to the director of the Museum of Morocco, a Moroccan genius, whom his admirers claim to have been the founder of algebra, devised the following symbols to correspond with the numerals from 1 to 0 as we now know them.

$$\Lambda Z 3 4 5 6 7 X 9 0$$

Now, apart from the fact that these symbols (or most of them) look very much like those we employ today, can you think of any hint you might get from the symbols themselves that would suggest to you which of the ten numbers we know each of them is likely to represent?

THE PROFESSOR'S ADDRESS

4. Professors are proverbially absent-minded: one of them once actually forgot the number of the house he was living in! It was, he remembered, in an ordinary suburban street, not particularly short and not particularly long, the houses being numbered consecutively from one upwards. The only other fact he recalled was that the total of all the house numbers lower than his was equal to the total of all the house numbers higher.

On the strength of just that much information can you deduce what must have been the number of his house?

A HOLIDAY OUTING

5. A motor coach can accommodate 30 passengers: the charge for the trip is 10s per head, with children at half price. Recently there was a full complement of passengers, and the takings were £1 less than they would have been if the numbers of adults and children had been reversed. How many children travelled on that occasion?

A JIGSAW PROVERB

6. Select three consecutive letters from each of the following ten words to make up a well-known proverb.

ABSOLUTE
ENTRENCH
POLICEMAN
KESTREL
ATHEIST
THEATRE
MORTGAGE
TROWEL
CHIFFON
UNDERSTAND

UNBELIEVABLE

7. Napoleon once met an old soldier with one arm. He stopped and asked him: 'Where did you lose your arm?'

'Sire, at Austerlitz,' was the reply.

'And were you not decorated?'

'No sire, I was forgotten.'

'Then,' rejoined Napoleon, 'here is my own cross for you. I make you *Chevalier.*'

'Ah sire,' exclaimed the soldier, 'Your Majesty names me *Chevalier* because I have lost one of my arms. What would your Majesty have done had I lost both of them?'

'I would have created you *Officier* of the Legion,' answered Napoleon.

Thereupon the soldier instantly drew his sword and

cut off his other arm.

If you are unable to credit this story, what is your reason?

DO YOU BELIEVE IT?

8. During a bridge match some time ago it was reported in the *Observer* (16 June 1968) that three identical hands were dealt in succession. Now do you believe it actually happened? And if not, why not?

TRANSPOSITIONS

9. A friend whose work necessitates checking the accuracy of the addition of large numbers of sums of pounds, shillings and pence tells me that the most frequent source of error is the transposition of figures; that is to say, the clerk has transposed the number of pounds and the number of shillings, the number of shillings and the number of pence, or the number of pounds and the number of pence. In other words, if the correct entry was £X Ys Zd, he may have written £Y Xs Zd, £X Zs Yd, or £Z Ys Xd.

If this has happened, then clearly the total would not amount to what it should be—there will be a difference either plus or minus. Naturally, for checking purposes, if one of these mistakes has been made it would be useful to know which kind of error it was.

Now assuming that there has been such an error, and only one such, and if you know the amount of the discrepancy in the total, can you think of any way of judging which of the three types of error has been made?

A DAMSEL IN DISTRESS

10. You probably know the legendary story of how Perseus, the Greek hero, rescued the beautiful Andromeda from a rock in the middle of a lake, where she was about to be devoured by a hideous dragon.

Now shall we try to reconstruct the story so as to make a puzzle out of it?

Andromeda was chained to this rock in the middle of a circular lake 100 feet in diameter; and Perseus, unhappily, was unable to swim. There was no boat available, but the hero was fortunately able to find a couple of planks of equal length. Alas! neither of them was long enough to reach from the edge of the lake to the rock, and there were no nails nor any means of lashing the planks together.

However, Perseus was as resourceful as he was bold, and he managed to go the damsel's rescue.

How did he do it? and what must have been the minimum length of the planks?

P.S. *The area of the rock was too small to need consideration.*

PERSEUS TO THE RESCUE AGAIN!

11. By a piece of really unpardonable carelessness Andromeda (see previous puzzle, 'A Damsel in Distress') again allowed herself to be captured and chained to that rock in the middle of the circular lake 100 feet in diameter. Once more Perseus sped to her rescue; but this time the two planks that had served him so well on the previous occasion had been removed. There were plenty of planks—five of them in fact, all equal in length—but they were appreciably shorter than the two he had found so useful; and of course there was no way of lashing them together.

However, once again the hero triumphed. What was his method, and what must have been the minimum length of the planks?

A QUESTION OF AGE

12. There is a gap of six years between the age of a man and that of his father-in-law. When the man is twice as old as his father-in-law is now, the latter will be 72. The man's age is *not* 27.

How old is he?

SPECIALLY FOR BILLIONAIRES

13. At the present time the value of the pound is about 2 dollars 40 cents, or, to put it another way, the dollar is worth about 8s 4d. Thus a million pounds here is worth about 2,400,000 dollars in the U.S.A. and a million dollars in the U.S.A. is worth about £417,000 here. But whereas a billion pounds over here is worth about 2,400,000,000,000 dollars in America, a billion dollars there is worth only about £417,000,000 in Britain.

Before starting to dabble in the money market perhaps it would be better to try to find out the reason for this discrepancy.

IN YOUR HEAD

14. Add up, in your head, all the numbers between 1 and 20 inclusive.

Well, perhaps not in your head. But what is the answer—and how did you arrive at it?

GENTLEMEN INCOGNITO

15. By what names are (or were) the following gentlemen better known?

(*a*) Henry Brodribb
(*b*) Muhammed Ali
(*c*) Samuel Clemens
(*d*) Giovanni Batista Montini
(*e*) Lord Verulam
(*f*) J. B. Morton

LADIES INCOGNITA

16. What are the names by which the following ladies are (or were) better known?

(*a*) Mary Ann Evans
(*b*) Mme. Margot de Arias
(*c*) Mrs M. E. L. Mallowan
(*d*) Mrs A. B. Connell
(*e*) Marie Louise de la Ramé
(*f*) Alice Marks

VERY QUICKLY, PLEASE!

17. How much is $67^2 - 33^2$?

A NICE EASY ONE

18. This problem is especially for Simon Haddon Squire, called Sammy. He is the young son of the lady who invented the Crossword Puzzles in this book, and he is exactly a year older than he was exactly a year ago.

In other words, Sammy is now ten, so I think he should be able to manage this one. *Also all my other readers of the same age.*

How many *odd* pairs of numbers add up to 14?

And how many *even* pairs add up to the same number?

D FOR WHAT?

19. I am thinking of three words beginning with the letter D which I want you to try to discover by adding a number of other letters. Crush the D and it becomes sorrowful; Set fire to it and it becomes happy; Separate it and it is with you no more.

What are the three words?

HALF A MOVE!

20. Do you agree that a book of this kind should have at least one chess problem? Nowadays, almost as many girls (and grown-up women) play chess as boys (and fully grown men).

Maybe chess was thought 'unladylike' in days gone by—but not any more. So this puzzle is for *any* of my readers (ladies, gentlemen, girls or boys) who may be interested. It is a much simplified version of a puzzle invented by a famous American problemist, Sam Loyd.

White to play, and mate in half a move! You heard what I said—in *half* a move!

Please, oh please, do not look at the solution at the end of the book until you have had a real try at solving this delightful little problem on your own.

A LADDERGRAPH

21. Change the word FISH to the word MEAT in *four* moves. You may alter only one letter at a time, and every time you must make a new word.

ODD MAN OUT

22. This kind of problem is a favourite of mine. I hope you like them too.

In each of the following lists there is one item which does not really 'belong'. What are they?

1. Priest, Monk, Dervish, Llama, Rabbi, Friar.
2. Piccolo, Trumpet, Flute, Triangle, Bugle, Flageolet.
3. Ant, Spider, Fly, Louse, Gnat, Moth.

SNAIL'S PROGRESS

23. A snail is crawling up a wall ten feet high. Every day he climbs three feet, but every night he slips back two feet. How long will it take him to reach the top?

NO NEED TO MEASURE

24. In this diagram the small square is precisely in the centre of the larger square which surrounds it.

Which of the four black triangles has the greatest area, and which the smallest?

DO YOU REMEMBER FARTHINGS?

25. Farthings are, of course, no longer legal tender. But supposing you had quite a lot of farthings—say 12,128 of them. Could you find anything significant about precisely *that* amount of farthings? What, for instance, would they have been worth?

A WORD SQUARE

26. In case you should not happen to know how to deal with a Word Square, just find five words to fill in this square which will read the same *down* as *across*.

I am giving you some clues of course.

	2	3	4	5
2				
3				
4				
5				

And here are the clues: (1) Mackerel bait; (2) Blab; (3) Artificial silk; (4) Make reparation; (5) Doctrine.

FOUR ODD COINS

27. A friend of mine told me that his two children had recently opened their money boxes, and that each

of them had two current coins, four *different* coins in all,
and yet each of them had exactly the same amount of
money. 'Isn't that strange?' he said.

'Not only strange,' I exclaimed, 'it's impossible!'

'Well,' replied my friend, 'perhaps I shouldn't have
said the same amount of money. More precisely, what
each of them had amounted to the same amount of
pennies.'

Now just what were the four coins those children
had?

ANOTHER LADDERGRAPH

28. Change MARE to FOAL in *five* moves. And
don't forget that in every move, changing only one
letter at a time, you have to make a *new* word.

A FINAL LADDERGRAPH

29. Finally a 'football treble', Change HOME to
DRAW in *nine* moves; and then change it to AWAY
in *ten* moves.

MIDDLE NAMES

30. What are the middle names of the following
well-known people?

    (*a*) Herbert ...... Wells
    (*b*) John .... Kennedy
    (*c*) Johann .... Bach

(*d*) Anthony .... Hawkins
(*e*) Franklin ...... Roosevelt
(*f*) Charles ..... Fox

ANOTHER WORD SQUARE

31. I warned you in the solution to the last one, did I not, that I was likely to find you another Word Square?
Here is the Square:

And here are the clues: (1) Herd; (2) Mature; (3) Suppose; (4) Poison; (5) Foe.
Remember that these words read the same *down* as *across*.

FOUR DIFFERENT ANSWERS

32. There are four two-digit numbers which, after you have multiplied each of them by 1¾, the result will be the original number with the digits reversed. If you find the smallest of these two-digit numbers, it should not be difficult to discover the other three.

BOY OR GIRL?

33. Here is an apparently very simple problem; but you must not dismiss it without thought.

(*a*) The elder of Mr Smith's two children is a girl. What is the probability that they are both girls?

(*b*) At least one of Mr Smith's two children is a girl. What is the probability that they are both girls?

(*c*) At least one of Mr Smith's twin children is a girl. What is the probability that they are both girls?

JUST A TOSS-UP

34. If you toss a penny three times, what are the chances that at least two heads will come up?

THE AGE DIVINER

35. In my first puzzle book I showed you how to discover a person's age. Now, in a rather more elegant version, you can get at the truth without him giving you any information at all. (Your victim must not be more than 32 years old.)

First prepare five cards such as those illustrated opposite—thin cardboard is the best to use.

Cut out the shaded portions; but, in the case of the fourth card, be careful to leave just enough at the corners of the cut-outs to ensure that the small white pieces do not fall out of the pattern.

YES

1		17
3		19
5		21
7		23
9		25
11		27
13		29
15		31

ON

YES

2		18
3		19
6		22
7		23
10		26
11		27
14		30
15		31

ON

YES

4		20
5		21
6		22
7		23
12		28
13		29
14		30
15		31

ON

YES

8		24
9		25
10		26
11		27
12		28
13		29
14		30
15		31

ON

Now you will require a Master Card, and you must get your victim to place the other five cards on top of it, one by one.

In each case, if his age appears on the card, it should be placed with the word 'YES' on top; if not, then with the word 'NO' on top.

You will find that just one number on the Master Card will be revealed—the number corresponding to his age!

Now the question is this: Can you design the Master Card? If not, you will find it in the Solutions at the end of the book.

WHO'S ZOO?

36. The owner of a Pet Shop has just bought 17 rabbits, 8 puppies and 34 kittens at a total cost of £38 5s 0d.

Last time, when prices were at the same level, he bought 13 rabbits, 39 puppies and 10 kittens for £46 16s 0d. The only other information I can give you is that each animal cost a round number of shillings.

From that information can you work out the individual prices of the rabbits, puppies and kittens?

YET ANOTHER WORD SQUARE

37. Can you take it? Five across and five down—the same words in each direction.

1	2	3	4	5
2	.			
3				
4				
5				

The clues are: (1) Beast of burden; (2) Conscious; (3) Heavenly food; (4) Sea eagles; (5) Minimum.

OBVIOUSLY?

38. The diameter of the surrounding circle is 2 inches. (Not actual size.)

What is the area of the *smaller* square?

THE GARDEN FÊTE

39. 'Can I go to the garden fête, dad?' a schoolboy asked his father. 'They've got five stands there, each one at a fixed price. At one stall everything costs 8*d*, at another 10*d*, at the third a 1*s*, at the fourth 1*s* 3*d*, and at the fifth 1*s* 6*d*.'

'All right,' replied his father. 'But I'm going to make one or two conditions. I'll give you a pound and expect you to spend it all and come back with 20 articles. But you must buy something at every stall—neither the same number of articles nor the same amount of money at any two stalls.'

This conversation was overheard by the schoolboy's younger brother.

'Can I go too, dad?' he asked.

'Well yes,' answered the generous parent. 'But only on the same conditions as your brother. And furthermore, I am going to make another condition. Neither of you must buy the same number of articles from any one stall, nor must you spend the same amount of money at any one stall.'

'Honestly,' remarked the elder boy to his brother, 'I'd just as soon stay at school for an extra period of arithmetic!'

However, they managed it. How?

THE TEMPLE OFFERING

40. When the leaders of the tribes brought their annual tributes to the Temple in Jerusalem, each sack, it was found, weighed an exact number of shekels. But the Temple treasurer, foolishly trying to save time, weighed them in pairs. The tributes brought by Abraham and Benjamin jointly weighed 8 shekels, he reported, those of Benjamin and Chaim together totalled 12 shekels, Chaim's and David's amounted to 13 shekels, while the total contributed by David and Ebenezer weighed just as much as those of Abraham and Benjamin together.

'But how,' asked the High Priest, 'am I to assess individual contributions?'

The treasurer stroked his beard in perplexity.

'The only other facts I can recall,' he said, 'are that all the weights were different, and that Ebenezer's sack was the lighest.'

Can you work out the individual contributions?

THE RAFFLE TICKET

41. 'I had high hopes of success when I saw that the number of the ticket I had bought in the Grand Totaliser-Plus Raffle was a perfect square,' said Jones. 'But alas! it didn't prove to be a winner, so I tore it in half meaning to throw it away. Just before I did so, however, I was interested to note that the two numbers into which I had accidentally divided it also formed perfect squares.'

'What a funny thing,' remarked Smith, 'because exactly the same thing happened to me.'

'Me too,' put in Robinson. 'But surely we can't all have drawn the same number!'

Of course they hadn't. But assuming that fewer than half a million tickets were issued, can you say what numbers were drawn by these three individuals?

NOTE. Raffle tickets are generally issued with the same number of digits on each ticket: that is to say, the number 18 will be printed as 000018. For the purposes of this puzzle, however, the numbers are assumed to have been printed in the ordinary way, so that eighteen would appear simply as 18.

WORDS OUT OF WORDS

42. The ever-popular pastime of making words out of words should really need no introduction. Everybody, except perhaps a few babies in prams, knows what you have to do.

When I was very young the most popular word for this game was 'Constantinople'. I do not know why, except that it is a good long name and you can make a lot of words out of it. Today, however, Constantinople is called Istanbul; so, if you like, you could try your hand at Istanbul after you have completed the task I am setting you now.

Actually there is no reason why only *one* word should be selected, and I have decided this time to choose three words, the title of this book: P U Z Z L I N G Y O U A G A I N. So you will treat 'Puzzling You Again' as one word, and you will try to discover how many other words you can find in it.

But there are certain rules you must observe, because every game requires a few rules to enable you to play it properly:

1. You may *not* use any proper names, either people or places.
2. You may *not* use any letter a second time unless

that letter appears twice in the words I have given you. (In fact there are two each of A, G, I, N, U and Z.)

3. You may *not* use words of two or even three letters, because it will make too big a total. (But perhaps you might like to know that, just for fun, I discovered 63 three-letter words!)

I suggest that you do not refer to a dictionary, but if you would care to check your result (as I did myself) I used *Chambers's Twentieth-Century Dictionary*.

Altogether (excluding two- and three-letter words) I got a grand total of 172.

So please have a go—particularly if it's a nasty wet day!

A RATHER GREEDY ONE

43. Two brothers returned from the village sweetshop with their mouths full and their pockets empty.

'D'you know, Dad,' said the elder, when his teeth had become more or less disengaged from the glutinous mass encumbering them, 'I bought five gobstoppers, seventeen dinkichocs and one fizzgog. They cost me 6s 3d.'

'Did you, indeed!' their father exclaimed. 'I hope your brother has been more economical.'

'Yes, I was, Dad,' replied the younger boy. 'I bought seven gobstoppers, three dinkichocs and four fizzgogs. I only spent 3s 4d.'

Then, somewhat to the children's astonishment, Father sent them off with his blessing and a renewed supply of pocket money. But after they had gone it occurred to him to wonder just how much apiece these delicacies had cost.

I didn't hear if he discovered the answer—but can *you* work it out?

MONEY-BOXES AGAIN

44. 'When my kids opened their money-boxes for Christmas,' remarked Jones, 'each of them had some half-crowns, some florins, some shillings and some sixpences—no other coins—and each child had precisely one pound in all.'

'Very interesting,' I said, 'but why are you telling me this?'

'Well, the curious thing was,' he added, 'that each child had just twelve coins, and no two had the same assortment of coins. Can you work out what those coins were?'

'Oh yes, I think so,' I replied. 'Of course, if you had more children it couldn't have happened.'

Can you say how many children there were and what their money-boxes contained?

POETRY BY NUMBERS

45. The figures from 0 to 9, in that order, stand for the letters spelling the name of an unpleasant affliction; each figure represents a particular letter.

Can you decipher this little verse about an unmusical clergyman?

612 830562 15629 612 813081'9 81742.
12 80729, 12 62509 179 1570;
179 12506 58129 59, 56 8107964596742
12 12509 769 43978 0502.

POSTMAN'S KNOCK

46. 'I think a "relief" postman must be working in our district,' said Jones. 'Robinson received a letter intended for Smith. The letter delivered to Smith ought to have gone to the man who got the letter that should have been left at the house where Thompson's letter arrived. And Thompson got the one intended for the man who received the one meant for the fellow who had Brown's put through his letter-box. There are only five of us living in the square, and we were all annoyed in this way.'

Who got whose letter?

... AND ALL THAT

47. 'How did you children get on in the history examination?' I asked.

'Not too badly,' answered Alfie, the eldest of the four. 'As a matter of fact, each of us scored the same number of marks, with five marks for every correct answer. We had to give the dates of important events, and all the questions were correctly answered by at least one of us.'

'I should hope so,' I said. 'Let's see your papers.' I looked at them and found that Alfie's answers were (*a*) 1588; (*b*) 1066; (*c*) 1649; (*d*) 1666. Bertie's replies were (*a*) 1649; (*b*) 1588; (*c*) 1066; (*d*) 1666. Charlie's list was (*a*) 1066; (*b*) 1649; (*c*) 1588; (*d*) 1666. Dickie's paper read (*a*) 1666; (*b*) 1649; (*c*) 1066; (*d*) 1588.

How many marks did each boy score, and what were the questions?

I WONDER WHY

48. What I am wondering is why so many of my younger readers seem to like my problems about food better than any other kind of problem. Well, it's none of *my* business!

Anyhow, here's a cookery one for you.

How long should it take you to make an omelette for, say, two people?

And how long should it take you to make scrambled eggs—also for two people? I mean the actual *cooking* time.

TALKING OF EGGS

49. Some time ago a lady wrote quite an interesting letter to *The Times*. She said: 'When boiling my family's eggs for breakfast I have noticed recently that they frequently stand on end in the water. When cut open the reason becomes obvious—they contain a large air pocket. This never used to be the case, and I would like to know who is to blame. The hen or the lion?'

Well, who *is* to blame? The hen, the lion—or could it be somebody else?

P.S. The lion, as you will know, has since disappeared.

A NICE CUP OF TEA

50. My local grocer tells me that he has just bought a parcel of 20 lb of tea, some China, some Indian, which cost him £7 13*s*. China tea costs a shilling a pound more than Indian. Had the quantities of each kind of tea been interchanged, he would have spent 6*s* less.

What is the price of each kind of tea, and how much of each did he buy?

WORDS OUT OF WORDS AGAIN

51. Well, I did warn you, did I not, that you might expect another of those awful word problems.

My previous one used the title of this book, so this time what about seeing how many words you can find in the name of its author? So try to discover as many words as you can in JONATHAN ALWAYS— with the same rules as last time.

But don't expect any help from the Solutions at the end of the book, because I just couldn't be bothered to do it myself. I did discover, however, that there are very few words in J O N A T H A N, and even fewer in A L W A Y S. Whereas, in using both names combined, there is an enormous number.

Actually I found 39 beginning with the letter A alone. And then I gave it up!

You can look immediately at the end of the book, if you wish; but I've already told you that you will get no help from it.

MAKING PICTURES

52. Most of my younger readers are still at school, of course; but some of you are no doubt already thinking about what you are going to do when you have finished your schooling and go out into the wide world. Maybe you will continue your training in some way or other and, I hope, improve your future prospects in the profession or trade of your choice.

Anyway, what I am wondering now is whether some of you will choose journalism as your career—and here is the reason.

One of the jobs that frequently falls to the lot of a picture editor on a newspaper or magazine is the selection and preparation of illustrations, and it is not as straightforward a task as you might suppose.

Having selected a suitable photograph you must then decide how to trim it; you may want to centralise your principal object, discard unnecessary bits of background or cloud, and so on.

When you have done all that you will have a picture of the right shape but probably not of the right *size*. You may want it to extend across one or perhaps two columns, and your photograph is not likely to be of exactly the right width. So you have to scale it up or (more probably) down.

Suppose, for example, you want a one-column picture, the width of your column being $2\frac{1}{2}$ inches, and that your trimmed photograph measures $6\frac{1}{2}$ inches in height and 4 inches in width. What will be the height of the actual picture you will use?

You can, of course, work this out by normal mathematical methods. Height divided by width must be a constant ratio; so by calling the height of your picture

x inches you get the equation $\dfrac{6\frac{1}{2}}{4} = \dfrac{x}{2\frac{1}{2}}$, or $\dfrac{13}{8} = \dfrac{2x}{5}$, so that $16x = 65$, and x will be $4\frac{1}{16}$ inches.

There is, however, a useful little dodge that picture editors employ in order to avoid these calculations.

First they draw a diagram of the exact size of the trimmed photograph and then mark in one diagonal, as shown below.

How do they then proceed, without doing any arithmetic at all, to find the height of the picture as it will appear in the paper?

TWO AND TWO

53. Two plus two equals four, and two multiplied by two also equals four.

Can you think of two *different* numbers that fulfil the same requirements—that is to say, which make the same total when added together as when multiplied?

MAGIC CIRCLE?

54. A circle has exactly the same number of inches in its circumference as it has square inches in its area.
What is its radius?

A SQUARE DEAL

55. An elderly lady had a square rug which she wished to cut up, and stitch some pieces together so as to make three square rugs.

Actually there are many ways in which she might have done this, but what you are asked to do is to find the only way in which she could achieve her purpose with just two straight cuts, and sewing together only two edges.

HENS AND THEIR HABITS

56. If a hen and a half lays an egg and a half in a day and a half, how many eggs will six hens lay in seven days?

NOTE. Please, I don't want anybody to write and tell me that they do not have a hen and a half!

TRY IT AND SEE

57. Can you break a matchstick with two fingers of one hand?
Try it and see!

SPEED—ANCIENT AND MODERN

58. In these days of jet propulsion, with new speed records for aircraft, racing-cars, speed-boats, etc., being won all the time, it may seem silly to talk about the speed of a cough. But is it?

And if you think I am asking a silly question, I am definitely not expecting a silly answer!

So what *is* the speed of a cough?

FOR MY YOUNGER READERS

59. London and Crewe are 158 miles apart.

A train travelling at 56 miles per hour leaves London for Crewe, and at the same moment a train travelling at 47 miles per hour leaves Crewe for London.

Which train is nearer to London when the two trains pass each other?

HOW LONG IS A YEAR?

60. There are several different kinds of year. For example, your mind will immediately leap to the Common year, having 365 days. Then there is Leap Year, with 366 days.

But what other kinds of year are there?

SOMETHING WITH DOMINOES

61. This problem is magic!

Invite two friends to play an ordinary game of dominoes; but while they are playing this game you must be outside the room.

Tell them to shout to you when they have finished—and you will then shout back to them the numbers at each end of the line!

How did you do it?

SHORT CUT TO FACTORISING

62. Do you know how, without going to the trouble of actually dividing, to find out whether a given number is divisible by 9 or 11?

AN UNFORTUNATE MUSICIAN

63. A certain violinist claimed that he could tame any wild animal merely by playing to it on his violin.

This proud boast was taken up by a local lion-tamer, who persuaded the violinist to substantiate his claim by playing to his own three man-eating lions. So the lion-tamer led the musician into the lions' cage, and the violinist started to play a beautiful melody.

Immediately one of the lions sat down to listen. Then another of the lions did likewise. But the third lion observed the violinist with angry eyes, and a few moments later sprang on him and ate him up.

'Why did you have to do that?' inquired one of the other lions of the lion who was now full of violinist.

What was the explanation of the lion, replete with violinist, to that perfectly reasonable question? Your answer should be equally reasonable, and entirely logical. You should, in fact, treat the question in just the same way as any other problem in this book.

PALINDROMES

64. The word M A D A M is a Palindrome because it reads the same backwards as forwards. No doubt you can think of some other examples.

But the best Palindromes are those which comprise a whole sentence (such as MADAM I'M ADAM!). If you are clever enough you may be able to discover one of these yourself.

At the end of the book I am printing a really excellent Palindrome. So look at it now if you want to, but I would prefer you to start on your own without reference to any further examples.

ALL ABOARD!

65. 'Any more for the *Skylark*?' shouted the boatman. 'Only six bob a head for the trip!'

'Well,' asked a prospective customer, 'if two more of us come will you take us all for five bob a head?'

'All right,' answered the boatman. 'I'll get just as much money if I do.'

How many people went aboard the *Skylark?*

KEEPING FIT

66. An athlete training for a walking match covered 154 miles, starting on a Sunday morning and finishing the following Saturday evening; and each day after the first he walked one mile farther than he had on the preceding day.

How many miles did he walk each day?

WHAT PRICE ORANGES?

67. 'Here you are, lady,' said the costermonger, 'finest oranges a shilling each or three for a half-crown.' One customer bought three, another bought one.

'Which is your better customer?' I asked him.

'Doesn't matter to me,' he answered. 'I make just the same profit on one deal as on the other.'

At what price did the dealer buy his oranges? And was his reply to me correct?

FREQUENCIES

68. We have already, at the beginning of this book, decided what letter in the alphabet occurs most frequently as the *initial* letter of words in the English language.

Now let us consider which letter in the alphabet occurs most frequently in English words.

Then, if you feel disposed, you could try to put some further letters in their order of frequency. Or *all* of them, if you like!

Finally, in the same connection, I want you to examine the following very carefully:

Can you find anything odd about this paragraph? You will not find anything wrong, but just odd. It is a good catch, although you can quickly find out what it is. So now you may start.

The answers to all the above questions are at the end of the book—but only after you have given due thought to these problems yourself.

SPOONERISMS

69. A Spoonerism, as you will know I am sure, is where there has been an accidental transposition of initial or other letters in a sentence, or of two or more whole words.

For instance, when the country parson told his wife that he was going for a little ride on his well-boiled icicle, she realised immediately that he was referring to his well-oiled bicycle.

You could now invent any number of similar Spoonerisms yourself—and at the end of the book I am giving you just one example in the form of a little anecdote.

MATCH-STICK WORDS

70. What *are* match-stick words anyway?

They are words that can be made with match-sticks, of course; that is to say they must be composed of letters which are *straight* and therefore not *curved*.

Take for example the title of this puzzle. 'Match' won't do, because the C is curved; 'Stick' won't do because the S is curved, and C appears again; 'Words' won't do because (apart from the reappearance of S) O, R, and D are also curved.

So what kind of word *does* satisfy our requirements? Well, here are a few examples, and after you have examined them you will of course be able to find a number of your own. A few more of mine are in the answers at the end of the book.

INFINITELY, INITIATIVE, FEMININITY, TWENTY-FIFTH, NINETY-NINTH, TITTLE-TATTLE.

Naturally the best prizes should go to the readers who find the *longest* words—but unfortunately there don't happen to be any prizes!

TOO MANY CIGARETTES

71. I have called this problem, 'Too Many Cigarettes' because I thought I ought to remind you that cigarette-smoking isn't very good for you anyway. That reminder, of course, is for my older readers; younger readers will know that the number of cigarettes they should smoke is exactly none!

Now for the problem! A man who saves his cigarette-ends finds that he can make a new cigarette out of seven stubs. He is going away on holiday during which he estimates that he will smoke 400 cigarettes.

How many cigarettes should he buy?

AN AMAZING WORD SQUARE

72. A friend sent me a Word Square of his own invention which he claims to be the 'biggest in captivity'! I think he may well be right because it contains as many as eight letters, and I have never seen one myself with more than seven. Usually they have only six or less.

I am going to give you the first and last words, and I want you to try to complete the Square yourself.

R	O	S	E	T	T	E	R
O							E
S							D
E							E
T							L
T							E
E							S
R	E	D	E	L	E	S	S

A rosetter, I understand, is someone who ties ribbons on chocolate-boxes, etc. 'Redeless' means without counsel or wisdom.

JUST SUPPOSING . . .

73. If you were to save a halfpenny in the first week of a year, a penny in the second week, twopence in the third week, and so on—doubling the amount every week for the whole year, how much would you save altogether?

The result is truly astonishing—and I would not recommend you to try to spend your total savings in one go.

HIDDEN WORDS

74. In my previous book I quite forgot to include any hidden words—which was a pity, because I think they are rather popular. I apologise if I find I am wrong.

Well, there's a hidden word in the last sentence I have written above. It is the name of a country, and all the letters are consecutive. What is it?

And here is the answer, which will show you what to do with the examples that follow:

I apologise if I fIND I Am wrong.   (India)

Now you can carry on:

1. This letter must be answered quickly. (A vegetable)
2. This boy is a little rascal, full of fun.   (An animal)
3. Of the very large meal, not a vestige remains. (An animal)
4. Living in a monarchy enables one to pay respects to the crown.   (Two of them—an animal, also a bird)
5. You are such a dreamer! I called you twice and you took no notice. (A country)

6. The castle at Windsor relies on its visitors' good behaviour.   (A plant)

MORE HIDDEN WORDS

75. 1. I like watching a fast flowing river from the tow-path, rushing away to the sea.   (A bird, also a plant)

2. When did he go? O, seven minutes ago.   (A bird, also a cereal)

3. Fruit won't ripen on a sunless wall owing to the coldness of the stones.   (A bird)

4. What is called offal consists of heart, liver, kidneys, etc.   (A bird, also an animal)

5. The ice is too thin. It should not be walked upon yet.   (Part of the body, also an animal)

6. A journey to the moon I would call a mad adventure.   (An animal)

7. The pastor knows every member of his congregation.   (A bird)

8. Children, you must go to bed—how late it is, Mother said.   (A bird, also an insect)

9. For some animals grass is best, oats for others. (An animal)

10. To advertise in the papers costs a lot of money. (Two animals)

11. What does one find in the ashpan? The remains of the fire.   (Two hidden animals and a tree)

12. The first time I went on ice I hardly dared to move, but with every step I grew bolder.   (A tree, a weight and an animal)

JUST IN TIME!

76. When is eleven o'clock not necessarily 11 A.M. or 11 P.M.?

SINGULAR PLURALS

77. I am using the word 'Singular' to mean 'unusual'; which, you must agree, is a correct use of the word. Many of our plurals are 'singular', and no doubt you will think this applies to at least some of the following dozen of them.

(*a*) Buffalo, (*b*) Calf, (*c*) Duck, (*d*) Goose, (*e*) Echo, (*f*) Dozen, (*g*) Gross, (*h*) Tax, (*i*) Taxi, (*j*) It, (*k*) Myself, (*l*) Jonathan Always.

ARE YOU RESOURCEFUL?

78. Supposing you wanted to break a length of string, and you hadn't scissors or a knife handy, how would you go about it?

A CATALYST

79. Put a lump of sugar in a saucer, strike a match, and try to set light to the sugar. You can't do it, can you?

But what is a catalyst? It is a substance which, without undergoing change itself, produces a chemical change in another body.

So can you think of a very simple catalyst that will enable you to set light to that lump of sugar?

IN THE KITCHEN

80. Sprinkle a little salt on the kitchen table. Then sprinkle a little pepper on top it.

Now separate the pepper from the salt!

You can't? Well, if you are absolutely sure you cannot do it you will have to turn to the answer at the end of the book.

AN ANAGRAM

81. Perhaps I first ought to explain that an Anagram is the transposition of the letters in a word, or words, which form a new word or words.

Now examine the following:

THE OXFORD AND CAMBRIDGE ANNUAL BOAT RACE

I want you to rearrange *all* the letters in the above to make a complete sentence which has a definite bearing on the subject.

There could be more than one answer to this problem, but I think you are unlikely to find a more satisfactory solution than the one you will refer to at the end of the book after you have experimented on your own.

RATHER INGENIOUS

82. The pupils at a certain school were faced with a mathematical problem which, oddly enough, was solved successfully by all the classical scholars, while the boys on the science side failed dismally. It was this:

Substitute numerals for letters to make the following a correct sum in multiplication.

$$
\begin{array}{r}
A\ B \\
A\ B \\
\hline
C\ B\ A \\
\hline
\end{array}
$$

SOMETHING SIMILAR

83. Whilst we still have the previous puzzle in mind, translate the following figures (and literals) into Roman numerals—and what do you get?

$$
\begin{array}{ccc}
100 & O & 500 \\
50 & I & 5ER \\
O & I & 50
\end{array}
$$

The answer will not be popular with most of my readers!

AND ANOTHER ONE

84. Can you correct this sum expressed in Roman numerals without altering any of the numerals or signs?

$$XI + I = X$$

DID HE MEET HIMSELF?

85. A man set off to walk up a mountain by a familiar path. His pace varied with the steepness of the climb, and sometimes he paused to admire the view. When he reached the top he spent the night at a hut situated there; and on the following morning he started off at exactly the same time as he had begun his climb the previous day to walk down the identical path. Once again his pace varied; once again he halted for short periods; and the downward journey did not take the same amount of time as the ascent.

Nevertheless, can we be sure that at some time during his return journey he found himself at exactly the same spot at precisely the same time as he had been on the previous day? And if the answer is 'yes', how would you prove it?

LIGHT-WEIGHT CONTEST

86. Those of you who read my book *More Puzzles to Puzzle You* may recall the problem in which the solver was supposed to have twelve coins identical in appearance, one of which, however, was slightly off weight (you were not told whether the false coin was light or heavy). What you were required to do was to find the false coin and state whether it was light or heavy after only three weighings and with no weights other than the coins themselves.

Here is a variation of the problem. The solver is confronted with 27 weights, marked 1 lb, 2 lb, and so on up to 27 lb. There is one false weight among them; but here we have the additional information that the weight in question is *light*. Otherwise the requirements are the same: detect the false weight in only three weighings and with no weights other than the 27 supplied.

THE CAPITALISTS

87.   John had twice as much in his pocket as had Joe; and if one-third of John's money had been added to one-quarter of Joe's it would have amounted to three-pence more than if one-quarter of John's had been added to one-third of Joe's.

So how much money did each of them have?

IT'S SIMPLY THIS

88.   Take the word THIS, and see how many complete sentences you can make out of the four letters it contains. You can use any of the letters as many times as you like.

No cheating, please! What I mean is that you mustn't look in the answers until you have tried to work it out for yourself.

You should discover *five* different sentences.

TIME IS MONEY

89.   A businessman travels occasionally from London to Manchester. He can go by express train which does the whole journey at an average speed of 60 miles an hour, or by excursion train (for which the fare is 2*d* a mile cheaper) which, including stops, travels at an average speed of 40 miles an hour. Reckoning the value of his time against money saved, he decides that he may just as well travel one way as the other.

At how much per hour does the man rate the value of his time?

SQUARING THE CIRCLE

90. 'Squaring the circle' is, as most of us know, a term used to describe an impossible task. The reason for this is that Euclid, using, as he did, only a straight-edge and a pair of compasses, was unable to construct a square of exactly the same area as that of a given circle. Nor has any later mathematician, confining himself to only these instruments, managed to solve the problem—in fact it has been proved to be impossible.

We can, however, using no mathematical instruments other than a pair of compasses and an ordinary school ruler, construct a square with an area *very nearly* equal to that of a given circle.

Bearing in mind that the area of a circle is πr (that is to say, the length of the radius multiplied by itself and again multiplied by a number called π, the approximate value of which is 3·1416), how would you set about constructing a square with an area very close to that of the circle shown above?

NOTE. π is the Greek letter corresponding to the English letter P. Frankly I have no idea why this particular Greek letter was chosen.

REVERSALS

91. Twelve multiplied by twelve is 144 (well, isn't it!); and 21 multiplied by 21 is 441. (Well, work it out!)

That is to say the figures are reversed throughout.

$$12 \times 12 = 144$$
$$21 \times 21 = 441$$

You see what I mean?

Now can you find another such pair of two-digit numbers? And is there perhaps an alternative answer?

REVERTING TO REVERSALS

92. What is the smallest number that is a multiple of itself reversed? And what is the smallest number that is a factor of itself reversed? Of course we exclude numbers which are identical when reversed—such as, for example, 343.

ONE IN NINE

93. Can you arrange the digits from one to nine in

three rows so that the first two numbers will add up to the third number?

And is there more than one possible answer?

ONE IN NINE AGAIN

94. Having solved the previous problem (one hopes!) can you now arrange the digits from one to nine in three rows making an addition sum, just as before, but with the proviso that the second number shall be double the first, and the third three times the first?

And could there, perhaps, be more than one answer to this?

A LITTLE UNUSUAL?

95. Can you see anything interesting about these figures?

$$\frac{1}{2} = \frac{2}{3} \times \frac{3}{4}$$

The sum, you will agree, is correct.

JUST A REARRANGEMENT

96. Here are 9 threes, arranged so that the three horizontal rows, the three vertical rows, and the two diagonal rows together amount to eight rows, each adding up to nine.

$$3 \quad 3 \quad 3$$
$$3 \quad 3 \quad 3$$
$$3 \quad 3 \quad 3$$

Can you rearrange these 9 threes so that they form *ten* rows, each row still adding up to nine?

CHINESE IN ONE LESSON

97. Can you read this?

This isn't Chinese
It's English.
Ha—ha!

Or *isn't* it Chinese?

A MATHEMATICAL MILKMAN

98. A milkman, with a churn almost full of milk, had two measures: one contained 5 pints, and the other 3 pints.

But a customer asked the milkman for only one pint of milk.

How did the milkman provide his customer with exactly one pint?

OUR MOTHER TONGUE

99.   Look at these two sentences, and I think you will agree that although they seemingly express complete opposites they do in fact mean exactly the same thing.

> Will you excuse me keeping my hat on?
> Will you excuse me taking my hat off?

Can you explain this?

A NICE EASY ONE

100.   A guest, on leaving his hotel, left £2 with the manager for distribution among those members of the staff who had particularly attended to his needs. He requested that the waiter who had regularly served him at table should receive 2s more than the chambermaid; that the chambermaid should be given 2s more than the hall porter; and the porter 2s more than the 'boots'.

After the guest had departed the manager, who was no mathematician, laboriously worked out how much should be alloted to each of the persons concerned—and in the end he arrived at the correct amounts.

What were the tips each member of the staff received?

ANOTHER EASY ONE

101.   Oh, so you like nice easy ones, do you? Then here's another of them. Smith shuffled two packs of playing cards; then, cutting the cards into two stacks, he picked up one of the stacks and counted the cards in his hand.

'How many cards do you hold in your hand?' asked his friend.

'Well', replied Smith, 'if I divide the number by 2, 3, 4, 5 or 6 I am left with one over every time.

How many cards had Smith in his hand?

FOR A WET DAY

102.   If it's raining, and you don't want to go out, you might care to amuse yourself by writing a short story (or even a few long sentences) in which every word begins with the same letter.

An easy letter to choose is the letter S, and at the end of the book I am printing a charming, old-fashioned example which was published in a magazine as long ago as 1897.

THIS IS MAGIC

103.   Hand somebody a pack of cards, and ask him or her (as the case may be) to shuffle them. Females are usually so clumsy at shuffling cards—so perhaps it had better be a male person!

Now take a table-knife and insert it *anywhere* in the pack, raising the corner a fraction of an inch. You can then tell your friend to his astonishment what card lies immediately above the knife.

How is it done?

SOMETHING IN COMMON

104. Examine these six words, and see if you can discover that they have a common characteristic.

DEFT, SIGHING, CALMNESS, CANOPY, FIRST, STUN.

And *don't* look at the end of the book—well, not yet. You can work it out, I am sure, if you try.

WHERE ARE YOU FROM?

105. A Londoner is, of course, someone who comes from London. But what do you call someone who comes from:

(*a*) Aberdeen; (*b*) Liverpool; (*c*) Manchester; (*d*) Glasgow; (*e*) Newcastle; (*f*) The Orkneys.

ANYTHING WRONG HERE?

106. Of the following sentences or phrases some are correct, some are incorrect. You are required to correct the incorrect ones. And you must try not to 'incorrect' the correct ones!

1. I am not so tall as him.
2. You are taller than I.
3. Were I to do so . . .
4. Either of the three.
5. Let each esteem others as good as themselves.
6. They ruined one another.
7. The two first . . .

8. The quality of the plums was excellent.
9. It was most unique.
10. I expected to have met you.
11. I should have thought that he would have come.
12. We accuse him for . . .

AND AGAIN

107. I seem to have a few more of those sentences and phrases for correction or otherwise—so shall we continue?

1. We acquit him from . . .
2. I didn't ought to have done it.
3. I am adverse to that.
4. I am small in comparison to you.
5. Adequate to . . .
6. We die of want.
7. I never work whenever I can help it.
8. Somehow or another . . .
9. I am averse from that.
10. Undeniable references required.
11. His opinions are approved of by all.

And finally, is this all right?

12. It's raining like anything.

WHAT'S THE TIME?

108. How many minutes is it to 3 o'clock if 20 minutes ago it was three times as many minutes past one?

A FINAL ODD MAN OUT

109. Which is the odd man out in each of the following lists?

1. Charles Dickens, W. M. Thackeray, George Eliot, Wilkie Collins, Anthony Trollope, George Meredith.
2. Elephant, Lama, Camel, Buffalo, Lion, Tiger.
3. Baal, Allah, Isis, Osiris, Thor, Zeus.

SOMETHING WITH MATCHES

110. I always have to do something with matches in my books, so this time you can turn these four matches into a square.

MATCHES AGAIN

111. How would you turn nine matches into ten?

NEARING THE END

112. You begin by writing with it in one syllable. Then you all but complete it with another three syllables. What is the word for it?

A KNOTTY PROBLEM

113. Borrow two friends! You can return them to themselves when you have finished this experiment.

Then, with a length of string, say about a yard long, tie the ends round the wrists of one of them.

Now, with another piece of string of about the same length, do the same thing to your other friend, with the second string passing through the first one, thus tying your friends together. The illustration will make this perfectly clear.

Now ask your friends to try to separate themselves without untying any of the knots and, of course, without cutting either of the pieces of string.

They will probably get into a terrible tangle—and meanwhile you will stand there laughing at them.

But it *can* be done—and really quite easily.

REMEMBERING NOT TO FORGET

114. This is really *another* knotty problem. Some people tie a knot in a handkerchief if they want to remember something—so here is a rather unusual way of tying a knot if you are interested to try.

Find a *large* handkerchief (or a face-towel or scarf), and place it outstretched on a table. Then fold your arms across your chest, either left over right or right over left, and now pick up two ends of the handkerchief with each hand.

Then, in that position, tie a knot in the handkerchief. Can you do it?

ANOTHER KNOTTY PROBLEM

115. Which of these drawings, if any, makes a knot?

A REPETITION

116. I included a problem in my previous book *Still More Puzzles to Puzzle You* which was unfortunately printed incorrectly. So here it is again, correct this time, with my sincerest apologies for the error.

Perhaps it may surprise you to know that we can construct a long division sum in which all the figures are represented by X's, and yet it is not too difficult to reconstruct it.

Here is the sum.

```
              ·  ·
            ·xxxxx
         ──────────
      xx)x
           xx
           ──
          xxx
          xxx
          ───
           xxx
           xxx
           ───
            xxx
            xxx
            ───
             x
```

For the benefit of those who do not already know it, I had better explain that a series of figures with dots over the first and last of them (as in the quotient here) represent a recurring decimal. That information is sufficient to enable you to reconstruct the whole sum.

SOLUTIONS

INITIALLY

1. Police Constable; Privy Council; Privy Councillor; *Patres Conscripti* (Conscript Fathers, enrolled as Roman Senators); Postcard.

In small letters it stands for: per cent; also postcard again.

Did anybody get all of them—including the Latin one?

INITIALLY AGAIN

2. The greatest number of English words begin with the letter S. And the smallest number begin with X.

Now, if you like, you could continue by placing other letters in their correct order. You can check your results with a dictionary.

MOROCCAN MATHEMATICS

3. Each of the symbols contains a number of angles corresponding to the number it represents. Thus, there are three angles in ⌇, seven in ⇥, and so on. The symbol O, being circular, of course contains no angles at all.

By the way, have you ever noticed how most continental people write the figure seven? It looks like this ⇁ , so I imagine it comes from the figure seven above.

THE PROFESSOR'S ADDRESS

4. The Professor lived at the house numbered 35 in a street of 49 houses.

If we call the number of the Professor's house x, and take the total number of houses in the street as being n, then the total of all the house numbers lower than his will be $1 + 2 + 3 + \ldots + (x - 1)$ which is equal to $\dfrac{x(x - 1)}{2}$; and the total of the numbers of the houses higher will be $(x + 1) + (x + 2) + \ldots + n$, which is equal to $\dfrac{n(n + 1)}{2} - x - \dfrac{x(x - 1)}{2} =$ $\dfrac{n^2 + n - x^2 - x}{2}$, and this we know must be equal to $\dfrac{x^2 - x}{2}$. Thus $2x^2 = n(n + 1)$.

To solve this we have to find pairs of consecutive numbers such that one is a perfect square and the other is double a perfect square. The lowest four pairs meeting this requirement are 1, 2; 8, 9; 49, 50; and 288, 289; giving the house numbers respectively as 1, 6, 35 and 204.

That he lives in house number 1 in a street consisting of one house is mathematically sound but not very sensible. A street of only eight houses is certainly a very short one, while 288 houses would constitute a long street. Hence the solution given is the only one that makes sense.

A HOLIDAY OUTING

5. There were 17 children.

Since x children paid $5x$ shillings and $(30 - x)$ adults paid $10(30 - x)$ shillings, the total receipts were $300 - 5x$ shillings.

Had the numbers been reversed, $(30 - x)$ children would have paid $5(30 - x)$ shillings, and x adults would have paid $10x$ shillings, a total of $150 + 5x$ shillings.

So $\qquad 150 + 5x - 20 = 300 - 5x$

Therefore $\qquad\qquad 10x = 170$

and $\qquad\qquad\qquad x = 17.$

A JIGSAW PROVERB

6. 'Absence makes the heart grow fonder.'

ABSolute
entrENCh
policEMAn
KEStrel
aTHEist
tHEAtre
moRTGage
tROWel
chifFON
unDERstand

UNBELIEVABLE!

7. If you really believe that story, you are capable of believing almost anything!

. The old soldier, as we know, had only one arm, so it was presumably with that arm that he drew his sword. Then did he cut off the arm which was holding the sword? Don't be ridiculous!

If the incident occurred in any form at all, which I strongly doubt, the old soldier might have asked Napoleon, or somebody else standing nearby, to cut off his remaining arm.

P.S. It may interest some of my readers to know that this very year (1969) is the bicentenary of both Wellington and Napoleon. Wellington was born in April 1769, and Napoleon in August of the same year. (Napoleon died in 1821, and Wellington in 1852.)

DO YOU BELIEVE IT?

8. Well, I don't! In the newspaper account of this affair it was stated that a 'mathematician and computer expert' had estimated that the odds against such a coincidence happening *once* were 27 thousand million trillion (27 and 27 noughts after it) to one. He added, we are told, that the chance of it occurring again were 'impossible to gauge mathematically'.

Not having a computer handy, I make the odds against *one* only such repetition as almost twice as much;* but one can't argue against a computer, can

* To be precise, 53, 644, 737, 765, 488, 792, 839, 237, 439, 999 to one!

one? And anyway the odds quoted would be high enough.

I do not quite know what this authority means by saying that the odds against a repetition are 'mathematically incalculable'. Clearly, if the odds against anything happening once are x to one, then the odds against its happening twice are x^2 to one, so that, accepting his figure, the odds against a repetition of this incident would be 729 followed by 54 Os to one; and for my part I would be prepared to take that as an impossibility.

What you may not have realised, however, is that the odds against *any* particular deal, including the one that you make right now, are exactly the same: no combination of 52 cards is any more or less unlikely than any other combination. So, however improbable it may be that a particular deal followed an identical one, it is no more unlikely than that a perhaps totally different deal *specified in advance* should occur. Pretty well anything that happens is exceedingly unlikely; yet it still does happen. But not (as we are asked to believe here) twice in succession!

Let us take a rather simpler proposition in the field of probabilities. Suppose you toss a coin: it is, you will agree, equally likely to come down heads as tails. If you toss again the probability is unchanged. But supposing you had thrown an uninterrupted series of twelve heads—wouldn't you think, if you were asked to forecast the result of the 13th spin, that it was now 'tails' turn? If you did think so you would be wrong. Coins have no memories; and the past (at any rate so far as tossing them is concerned) cannot affect the future. Your chances of throwing a head remain unaffected however often you have done so before.

TRANSPOSITIONS

9. If the pounds and shillings figures have been interchanged, then the sum representing the discrepancy will of course show nought in the pence column and the pounds and shillings figures will add up to 19. If shillings and pence have been transposed then there will be no pounds in the discrepancy figure and the shillings and pence figures will total 11. If the pounds have been interchanged with pence, then the shillings figure will be 19 and the pounds and pence figures will total 11. Here is an example:

	£	s	d		£	s	d		£	s	d
Correct entry:	11	6	9		11	6	9		11	6	9
Erroneous entry:	6	11	9		11	9	6		9	6	11
Discrepancy:	4	15	0	—	2	9		1	19	10

P.S. As a matter of interest, and not entirely irrelevant to this problem, have you ever noticed that in the case of £6 13s 0d, if you reverse the pounds and shillings figures you exactly double the amount? That is the only sum of money to which this applies.

A DAMSEL IN DISTRESS

10. Perseus placed his two planks as shown in the diagram.

Call the length of each plank x feet. Then in the triangle ABC, AB = 50, AC = x and BC = $\dfrac{x}{2}$

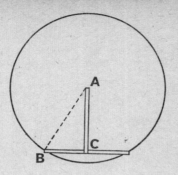

So $x^2 + \dfrac{x^2}{4} = 2500$

and $x^2 = 2000$

Thus $x = 44\cdot72$ approximately; allowing a little space for overlapping, say 45 feet.

PERSEUS TO THE RESCUE AGAIN!

11. Perseus arranged the planks as shown in the diagram.

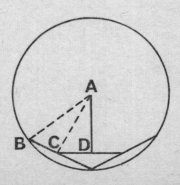

Let the length of each plank be x feet. Then in the triangle ABC AB $= 50$, BC $= \dfrac{x}{2}$

So $\qquad$ AC^2 = AB^2 − BC^2 = 2500 − $\dfrac{x^2}{4}$

In the triangle ACD

$$AC^2 = 2500 - \frac{x^2}{4}, \quad AD = x, \quad CD = \frac{x}{2}$$

So $\qquad\qquad$ 2500 − $\dfrac{x^2}{4}$ = $x^2 + \dfrac{x^2}{4}$

Thus $3x^2 = 5000$, and $x = 40 \cdot 8$ approximately.

Again allowing something for overlapping, the planks must have measured 41 feet each.

A QUESTION OF AGE

12. He is 45—and his father-in-law is 39. But why?

If we assume (but why should we?) that the father-in-law is older than his son-in-law then we may take it that the son-in-law's age in years is x, and the father-in-law's is x plus 6. When the son-in-law is twice as old as his father-in-law is now, his age will be $2(x + 6) = 2x + 12$, an increase of $x + 12$ years, so the father-in-law's age will be $x + 6 + x + 12 = 2x + 18 = 72$. So $2x = 54$, and $x = 27$.

But we are told that the son-in-law's age is *not* 27. So the father-in-law must be six years *younger* than his son-in-law, that is to say the son-in-law's age in years is x, and the father-in-law's is $x − 6$. When the son-in-law

is twice as old as his father-in-law is now, he will be $2x - 12$, an increase of $x - 12$, so the father-in-law's age will be $x - 6 + x - 12 = 2x - 18 = 72$. So $x = 45$ (the son-in-law's age), and the father-in-law is 39.
So there we are!

SPECIALLY FOR BILLIONAIRES

13. The reason for this startling difference is that whereas a billion in this country is 1,000,000,000,000, (a million millions), a billion in America—and in France too, for that matter—is only 1,000,000,000 (a thousand millions).

IN YOUR HEAD

14. The answer is 210.
The sum of any series of whole numbers from 1 upwards, say from 1 to n, is $\dfrac{n(n+1)}{2}$.

In this case, $\dfrac{20 \times 21}{2} = 210$.

GENTLEMEN INCOGNITO

15.
(a) Henry Irving
(b) Cassius Clay
(c) Mark Twain

(d) The Pope (Paul VI)
(e) Francis Bacon
(f) Beachcomber

LADIES INCOGNITA

16.
(a) George Eliot
(b) Margot Fonteyn
(c) Agatha Christie
(d) Ninette de Valois
(e) Ouida
(f) Markova

VERY QUICKLY, PLEASE

17. The answer is 3,400.
The difference between two squares, say x^2 and y^2, is $(x + y)(x - y)$. In this case we have $(67 + 33)(67 - 33) = 100 \times 34 = 3400$.

A NICE EASY ONE

18. Odd pairs, 4. Even pairs, only 3.
NOTE. A few words of grand stuff by way of explanation! If a number (n) is divisible by 4, then it can be made up of $\frac{n}{4}$ pairs of even numbers and $\frac{n}{4}$ pairs of odd numbers. If it is not divisible by 4, then it can be

made up of $\dfrac{n-2}{4}$ even numbers and $\dfrac{n+2}{4}$ odd numbers. *See?*

D FOR WHAT?

19. D-pressed, D-lighted, D-parted.

HALF A MOVE!

20. First of all, what *is* half a move? Every move in chess is complete in itself with only one exception, namely in castling, in which the player first shifts his king (half a move) and then moves the rook to the other side of it.

Here the previous position was that the white king occupied its own square. White moved it to K Kt square (half the operation of castling), thus producing the position shown. Now he carries out the other half of the move by transferring the rook to K B square.

And Black is mated!

A LADDERGRAPH

21.
                FISH
                FIST
                FIAT
                FEAT
                MEAT

Perhaps you have thought of another way of doing it?

ODD MAN OUT

22. 1. They are all ministers of religion except LLAMA, which is an animal.

2. They are all wind instruments except TRI-ANGLE, which is a percussion instrument.

3. They are all insects except SPIDER, which is an arachnid.

SNAIL'S PROGRESS

23. Eight days. At the end of seven days he will have climbed seven feet, and he will progress the remaining three feet on the eighth day. Whether he then slips back two feet or not doesn't matter; he will at any rate have attained his objective.

NO NEED TO MEASURE

24. The areas of all the four triangles are exactly the same. In every case the base of the triangle is a side of a smaller square, and its altitude is the difference between one side of the larger square and one side of the smaller.

Since the area of a triangle is $\dfrac{\text{base times altitude}}{2}$, it is clear that they must all be the same.

DO YOU REMEMBER FARTHINGS?

25. 12,128 farthings amount to exactly £12 12s 8d, which are the same figures in the same order. There is no other number of farthings that would produce that result—although to prove it is not very easy. But for any really brilliant reader who would be interested in the proof, here it is.

Since the number of farthings in a pound is nearly 1000 (actually 960) it is clear that there must be three digits to follow after the number of pounds, so that there must be a double figure either in the shillings column or the pounds column. But since there are four farthings to a penny, the number of pence must be either four or eight, so that the double figure must be in the shillings column. Hence the sum of money may be written as:

$$\pounds \quad s \quad\quad d$$
$$x \quad 10 + y \quad 4 \text{ or } 8$$

When this is written out as a complete number, therefore, it will be $1,000x + 100 + 10y + 4$ or 8. And when it is expressed as farthings it will be $960x + 480 + 48y + 16$ or 32. So that $1,000x + 10y + 104$ or $108 = 960x + 48y + 496$ or 512. Therefore $40x - 38y = 392$ or 404, or $20x = 19y + 196$ or 202.

Clearly y is even, so that $19y$ must equal 38, 76, 114 or 152. As $19y + 196$ or 202 is a multiple of 20, neither 76 nor 152 will meet the case. So that either $20x = 38 + 202$, giving $x = 12$ (the correct answer), or else $20x = 114 + 196 = 310$, which is not a multiple of 20. Thus $x = 12$, and 12,128 farthings make £12 12s 8d.

Is anybody still *with* me?

A WORD SQUARE

26.

I trust you solved that one, because I wouldn't be surprised if I produced at least one more of these before I get to the end of the book.

FOUR ODD COINS

27. One child had one (old) penny and a new ten-penny piece; and the other had a new fivepenny piece and a sixpence.

Thus each had a total of eleven pennies (old and new), although of course the sums were not of the same value—the first being worth (in old currency) 2s 1d and the second 1s 6d.

P.S. Actually those children spent all that money, but at the time of writing their money-boxes are quite heavy, and they rattle like anything!

ANOTHER LADDERGRAPH

28.
MARE
FARE
FORE
FORM
FOAM
FOAL

Can you improve on it, I wonder?

A FINAL LADDERGRAPH

29.
HOME
TOME
TIME
TILE
TILL
TELL
TEAM

TRAM   SEAM
DRAM   SWAM
DRAW   SWAY
                AWAY

MIDDLE NAMES

30. (*a*) George; (*b*) Fitzgerald; (*c*) Sebastian; (*d*) Hope; (*e*) Delano; (*f*) James.

ANOTHER WORD SQUARE

31.

D	R	O	V	E
R	I	P	E	N
O	P	I	N	E
V	E	N	O	M
E	N	E	M	Y

Just to annoy, I may possibly give you at least one more of these!

FOUR DIFFERENT ANSWERS

32. Here they are—all four of them.

$$12 \times 1\tfrac{3}{4} = 21$$
$$24 \times 1\tfrac{3}{4} = 42$$
$$36 \times 1\tfrac{3}{4} = 63$$
$$48 \times 1\tfrac{3}{4} = 84$$

And there are no others.

BOY OR GIRL?

33. (*a*) Evens (or $\tfrac{1}{2}$). The only possibilities are girl–girl and girl–boy.

(*b*) Two to one on (or $\tfrac{2}{3}$). The possibilities here are girl–girl, girl–boy, and boy–girl.

(c) You may think this rather a cheating question. Its terms do not seem to differ materially from those stipulated in (b). But if the twins are identical (by no means an unlikely event) they *must* be both girls. So here the probability is in excess of $\frac{2}{3}$; but, of course, one would need to have statistics about the likelihood of the occurrence of twins (identical or not) in a particular family.

JUST A TOSS-UP

34. The chances are precisely equal. Clearly in tossing a coin three times you *must* have a majority either of heads or tails; and it is equally as likely to be one as the other.

It we list all the possibilities, they are:

	1	2	3	4	5	6	7	8
Throw No. 1	H	H	H	H	T	T	T	T
Throw No. 2	H	H	T	T	H	H	T	T
Throw No. 3	H	T	H	T	H	T	H	T

You have a majority of heads in columns 1, 2, 3 and 5, which is four out of eight, or a fifty-fifty chance.

THE AGE DIVINER

35. Here is the Master Card—but I hope you did not need it.

MASTER CARD

29	17	28	16
31	19	30	18
21	25	20	24
23	27	22	26
5	9	4	8
7	11	6	10
13	1	12	36
15	3	14	2

And it WORKS, does it not?!

WHO'S ZOO?

36. The rabbits cost 11 shillings each; the puppies, 17 shillings; and the kittens, 13 shillings.

From the two equations:

$$17x + 8y + 34z = 765$$
$$13x + 39y + 10z = 936$$

you can see that y must be a multiple of 17 and z a multiple of 13. But if y is as great as 34 the second equation is impossible, and if z is as great as 26 the first one is impossible. Hence $y = 17$, $z = 13$, and x is easily found to be 11.

YET ANOTHER WORD SQUARE

37.

C	A	M	E	L
A	W	A	R	E
M	A	N	N	A
E	R	N	E	S
L	E	A	S	T

So that will do with that!

OBVIOUSLY?

38. One square inch.

Obviously the diameter of the circle is also the diagonal of the larger square. So that one side of the larger square is $\sqrt{2}$ inches. Call a side of the smaller square x inches. Then in any one of the right-angled triangles we have $2x^2 = (\sqrt{2})^2 = 2$.

So $x = 1$, and therefore the area of the smaller square is obviously 1^2, or one square inch.

THE GARDEN FÊTE

39. One boy bought 4 articles at 8d, 7 at 10d, one at 1s, 6 at 1s 3d, and 2 at 1s 6d, making a total of 20 articles costing 2s 8d + 5s 10d + 1s + 7s 6d + 3s = £1.

The other boy bought 2 articles at 8d, 5 at 10d, 8 at
1s, 4 at 1s 3d, and one at 1s 6d, also making a total of
20 articles costing 1s 4d + 4s 2d + 8s + 5s + 1s 6d =
£1.

Actually there are other solutions by interchanging
some of these figures.

THE TEMPLE OFFERING

40. Abraham's sack weighed 3 shekels, that of
Benjamin 5, Chaim's 7, David's 6 and Ebenezer's 2.

We have four equations with five unknowns:

$$A + B = 8 \qquad C + D = 13$$
$$B + C = 12 \qquad D + E = 8$$

From these it is easily seen that $B = 8 - A$, $C =
A + 4$, $D = 9 - A$, and $E = A - 1$. Since A's was
not the smallest contribution it cannot have weighed
less than 2 shekels, and since he and B together contributed 8 it cannot have been more than 6.

So the following distributions are possible:

	(1)	(2)	(3)	(4)	(5)
A	2	3	4	5	6
B	6	5	4	3	2
C	6	7	8	9	10
D	7	6	5	4	3
E	1	2	3	4	5

In column 5, E's figure is not the smallest; and
columns 1, 3 and 4 each give two sacks of the same
weight. Hence column 2 is the only one to satisfy the
data.

THE RAFFLE TICKET

41. The raffle tickets drawn by three individuals
were 49, 1681 and 225,625.

$$49 = 7^2 \qquad 4 = 2^2 \qquad 9 = 3^2$$
$$1,681 = 41^2 \qquad 16 = 4^2 \qquad 81 = 9^2$$
$$225,625 = 475^2 \qquad 225 = 15^2 \qquad 625 = 25^2$$

WORDS OUT OF WORDS

42. I imagine you feel a bit frustrated because,
although there are fifteen letters altogether in
P U Z Z L I N G Y O U A G A I N there are only
ten *different* letters. And there aren't enough important
letters like E or S. Sixteen of the twenty-six letters do
not appear at all!

Even so, the total I gave you of 172 isn't too bad, I
feel, and I have listed them here alphabetically:

A. Again, Aging, Agila (eaglewood), Agin, Agio
(financial term), Agog, Agoing, Agony, Ailing, Alga
(seaweed), Align, Along, Anal (from anus), Analogy,
Anan (failure to understand), Angina (medical), Anil
(indigo), Anna (Indian or Pakistani coin), Annal (a
year's entry in chronicle), Annoy, Annual, Annul,
Anoa (small buffalo), Anon, Apay (to satisfy, *archaic*),
Apian (of bees), Aula (a hall), Azilian (period of pre-
historian culture).

G. Gaga, Gain, Gainly, Gala, Gail (botanical),
Galop (lively dance), Gaun (going or gone, *Scots*),
Gaup (gape, provincial), Gazon (turf used in forti-
fication), Gila (venomous lizard), Gipy (boisterous
girl, *Scots*), Gagal (Indian Ox), Goal, Goanna, (large
lizard, Australian), Going, Guan (American bird),

Guano (manure), Gula (part of throat), Gulp, Gunny (jute fabric).

I. Iguana (tropical lizard), Ingan (onion, *Scots*), Inion (biological), Inlay (insert), Inly (inward), In-play (may be played), Inula (botanical), Inulin (from Inula), Inyula (S. African Antelope).

L. Lagan (Wreckage, also Ligan), Lain (from lay), Lana (genipap wood, S. America), Lang (long, *Scots*), Lanugo (Soft coat of hair), Lazy, Liana (any climbing plant), Liang (Chinese ounce), Ling (a fish), Lingo, Lingua (the tongue), Linin (scientific), Lining, Linn (waterfall), Lion, Loan, Logan (rocking stone), Loin, Long, Longan (a tree), Loup (leap, *Scots*), Lung, Lungi (loincloth), Lupin, Lying, Lyon (chief Herald of Scotland).

N. Naga (indian snake), Nain (own, *Scots*), Nazi (Nat.-Socialist, Hitlerite Germany), Nipa (E. Indian palm), Noggin, Nopal (Central American Cactus), Noun, Noup (a crag), Noyau (a liqueur), Nyanza (a lake), Nylon.

O. Ogling, Ogpu (former Russian secret police), Only, Opal.

P. Pagan, Pail, Pain, Palay (Ivory tree, S. Indian), Pali (sacred language, Buddhists), Paling (from pale), Pang, Pangolin (ant-eater, Asia, Africa), Paola (Papal coin, *obs.*), Paoli (plural of Paola), Paul (same as Paola, also follower of Paul of Samosita), Piazza (square or market-place), Pilau (Eastern rice dish), Pili (a nut), Pina (a cloth), Ping, Pining, Pinion, Pinna (a part of leaf, kind of mussel), Pinny (short for pinafore), Pinon (pine-seed), Piny (of pine trees), Pioy (firework, *Scots*), Pixy (Pixie), Plagal (musical term), Plain, Plan, Play, Playing, Ploy (occupation), Plug, Pong (to gag, slang), Pony, Poon (Indian tree),

Pugil (a pinch, formerly a boxer), Pulo (silky fibre), Punalua (Group marriage, Hawaiian), Puny, Punily (from puny), Puzzling, Puzzolana (volcanic dust), Pygal (belonging to the rump), Pylon, Pyoning (pioneer work).

U. Ugly, Ulna (bone in forearm), Unau (two-toed sloth), Ungainly, Ungula (a hoof, *zoological;* section of cylinder, *geom.*), Unio (kind of mollusc), Union, Upgo (go up), Uvula (at back of tongue).

Y. Yang (species of tree), Yaup (hungry, *Scots*), Yoga (Hindu philosophy), Yoni (Hindu symbol), Young, Yowl (to howl), Yuan (Chinese dollar), Yuga (one of the Hindu ages of the world), Yulan (Chinese flower).

Z. Zany (clown), Zigzag, Zizan (tzigany, Hungarian gipsy), Zinnia, Zigania (genus of grasses), Zona (zone), Zonula (small zone), Zulu, Zupa (village communities in early Serbia), Zupan (governor of Zupa), Zygal (see Zygon), Zygon (connecting bar).

So that's that at last! And I now only need to remind you that I suggested you might be interested to do the same with I S T A N B U L .

But at the same time I ought to warn you that I may well give you *another* Words Out of Words before you get to the end of these problems!

A RATHER GREEDY ONE

43. The gobstoppers cost $2\frac{1}{2}d$ each; the dinkichocs $3\frac{1}{2}d$, and the fizzgogs $3d$.

If you assumed that because each boy spent an exact number of pence, therefore each sweetmeat must also have cost an exact number of pence, you may have run into trouble.

Since farthings are no longer legal tender, each sweetmeat must, however, have cost an integral number of halfpence. So

$$5x + 17y + z = 150$$
$$7x + 3y + 4z = 80$$

Eliminating z, we arrive at the equation $x + 5y = 40$. Thus x must be a multiple of 5. But if $x = 10$, $y = 6$, so $7x + 3y = 88$, and the younger boy could not have got his sweets for 3s 4d. Hence $x = 5$, $y = 7$, $z = 6$.

MONEY-BOXES AGAIN

44. We are told that each child had 'some' coins of each value, so that distributions including only one coin of a particular value are excluded. The only possible assortments are 5 half-crowns, 2 florins, 2 shillings and 3 sixpences; 4 half-crowns, 3 florins, 3 shillings and 2 sixpences; and 2 half-crowns, 6 florins, 2 shillings and 2 sixpences. Thus there were three children.

You should have reached the answer by trial and error.

POETRY BY NUMBERS

45. The keyword is RHEUMATICS, and the verse reads:

> The curate hates the church's chime.
> He cries, he tears his hair;

His heart aches as at Christmastime
He hears its music rare.

The cryptogram is solved by making a number of inferences.

In line 1 the figure 9 follows an apostrophe; it is clearly S. Thus in line 3, 59 is either AS, IS or US, so that 56 must be AN, AT, IN, IT, or UP. So 5 is A, I or U, 6 is N, T or P. In the last line the combination 769 is therefore xNS, xTS or xPS. Clearly it must be ITS, so we now have the identities 7 I, 6 T and 9 S. The first word in the verse, 612, is thus a three-letter word beginning with T, and also the two-letter combination 12 appears alone several times. It is a reasonable probability, therefore, that the two words are THE and HE, giving 1 H, 2 E. Next we have as the second word in the third line HExxT and as the second word in the fourth line HExxS, so it may be presumed that the numbers 5 and 0 stand for A and R respectively.

Now for the entire word (meaning 'an unpleasant affliction') we have

0	1	2	3	4	5	6	7	8	9
R	H	E			A	T			S

and we can jump to RHEUMATICS right away.

POSTMAN'S KNOCK

46. Jones received Thompson's letter, Thompson Robinson's, Brown Jones's, Robinson Smith's, and Smith Brown's.

... AND ALL THAT

47. Each boy scored ten marks. The test paper asked for the dates of (*a*) the Spanish Armada; (*b*) the execution of King Charles I; (*c*) the battle of Hastings; and (*d*) the Great Fire of London.

Since every question has been correctly answered at least once, it follows that the four dates given are the correct ones; it remains only to place them in order.

To question one four different answers are given, one of which must be correct. The answer to question four must be either 1666 or 1588. If it is 1666, then Dickie's fourth and first answers are wrong, and his two remaining answers must either be both right or both wrong. It follows that Dickie (and therefore everybody) has scored ten marks. If the answer to the fourth question is 1588, then Alfie's first and last replies are wrong, so that his second and third answers must be right.

Since eight questions in all have been answered correctly, there must be one correct reply to question one, two to question two, two to question three, and three to question four.

The rest is easy.

I WONDER WHY

48. An omelette: approximately thirty seconds.

Scrambled eggs: approximately ten minutes—or twenty times as long.

No wonder your omelettes and scrambled eggs aren't always as successful as they ought to be!

TALKING OF EGGS

49. The hen is to blame because she laid the eggs perhaps three or four weeks before she ought to have done.

No, I'm only joking! What I really mean is that there has been a delay of three or four weeks in getting the new-laid eggs to the shops. Meanwhile the air-pockets form, and the eggs stand upright in the boiling water. Fresher eggs lie in the water slant-wise—and really new-laid ones lie down obediently.

A NICE CUP OF TEA

50. He bought 13 lb of China tea at 8*s* per lb, costing £5 4*s*, and 7 lb of Indian at 7*s*, costing £2 9*s*, a total of £7 13*s*. Had he bought 7 lb of China at 8*s* and 13 lb of Indian at 7*s* his total cost would have been £2 16*s* + £4 11*s* = £7 7*s*.

WORDS OUT OF WORDS AGAIN

51. Am I wasting your time? Perhaps you will think so if only because my *real* name may not be Jonathan Always after all!

MAKING PICTURES

52. All the picture editor has to do is to measure out a distance of $2\frac{1}{2}$ inches along the base line from the point D (the left-hand bottom corner), then draw a line parallel with one of the upright lines to cut the diagonal at the point E, and draw another line from that point parallel with the base. The smaller rectangle (with diagonal DE) will then give the exact dimensions of the picture as it will appear.

But why? Because, as you will readily see, if you take *any* point on the diagonal BD and join it by perpendiculars to the two sides you will have a rectangle of precisely the same *shape* as the original larger one. Since it is of the same shape, the ratio of the height to width must be the same; so what we have done is in fact to *construct* our first equation in visible (and measurable) form.

TWO AND TWO

53. There is no solution in whole numbers, but an infinite number if we allow the use of fractions. One of the two numbers can be anything you like. The second must be the first number divided by a number one less than itself. For example, 3 and $\frac{3}{2}$ will do, or 4 and $\frac{4}{3}$.

$$3 + \frac{3}{2} = 3 + 1\frac{1}{2} = 4\frac{1}{2}$$

$$3 \times \frac{3}{2} = 3 \times 1\frac{1}{2} = 4\frac{1}{2}$$

$$4 + \frac{4}{3} = 4 + 1\frac{1}{3} = 5\frac{1}{3}$$

$$4 \times \frac{4}{3} = 4 \times 1\frac{1}{3} = 5\frac{1}{3}$$

MAGIC CIRCLE?

54. The radius is 2 inches.

The area of a circle is πr^2 and the circumference is $2\pi r$. Since these two are equal we can divide each by πr, and we are left with $r = 2$.

A SQUARE DEAL

55. She marked a point x one-third of the distance along the top edge; and another, point y, one-third of the distance up one side, and cut twice as shown in this illustration.

She then had only to sew the two pieces marked A together (on the long sides) to form the third square.

Assuming the original rug to have measured three yards along each side (total 9 square yards) there would be one small square with a side of one yard, one with a side of two yards, and two pieces which when sewn together would make another square with a side of two yards ($1^2 + 2^2 + 2^2 = 9$).

HENS AND THEIR HABITS

56. Twenty-eight eggs. Thus:

$1\frac{1}{2}$ hens lay $1\frac{1}{2}$ eggs in $1\frac{1}{2}$ days
therefore $1\frac{1}{2}$,, ,, 1 egg in 1 day
  ,,   6 ,, ,,   4 eggs in 1 day
  ,,   6 ,, ,, 28 ,, ,, 7 days.

TRY IT AND SEE

57. Grip one end of the match in the fold of the first finger so that the other end rests on the side of your thumb.

Press your finger *downwards*, and your thumb *upwards*
—and there you are!

If you didn't get that one I almost despair of you!

SPEED—ANCIENT AND MODERN

58. At the height of a cough, when air is being forced
most rapidly out of the throat, its speed through the
throat is approximately 760 miles per hour. Not bad
going, you will agree!

Now you must excuse me for a moment before we
start on the next problem, while I clear my throat—at
approximately 760 miles per hour!

FOR MY YOUNGER READERS

59. The two trains are exactly the *same* distance from
London of course!

Didn't you get it—you silly thing!

HOW LONG IS A YEAR?

60.
1. The LUNAR year (354 days).
2. The SOLAR year (365 days, 5 hours, 48 mins.,
   46 secs.).
3. The GREGORIAN year (365 days, 5 hours,
   49 mins., 12 secs.).
4. The JULIAN year (365¼ days).
5. The SIDEREAL year (365 days, 6 hours, 9 mins.,
   9 secs.).
6. The ANOMALISTIC year (365 days, 6 hours,
   13 mins., 49·3 secs.).

SOMETHING WITH DOMINOES

61.   Before you give your friends the set of dominoes, secretly remove one of them and put it in your pocket. Do not, however, select a double, such as a double 1 or double 2.

When the game is completed the numbers at each end of the line will be the same numbers as those on the domino you have secretly removed!

SHORT CUT TO FACTORISING

62.   Add all the digits together, and if the resulting total is divisible by 9 so is the original number.

To test for divisibility by 11 take the two sets of alternate digits and, if they make the same total or differ by a multiple of 11, then the original number is divisible by 11.

Take, for example, the number 572,517.

$5 + 7 + 2 + 5 + 1 + 7 = 27$. So the number is divisible by 9.

$5 + 2 + 1 = 8; 7 + 5 + 7 = 19; 19 - 8 = 11$. So the number is divisible by 11.

Or again, take the number 5,091,867.

$5 + 0 + 9 + 1 + 8 + 6 + 7 = 36 = 4 \times 9$, so the number is divisible by 9.

$5 + 9 + 8 + 7 = 29; 0 + 1 + 6 = 7$; with the difference of 22 (twice eleven), so that the number is divisible by eleven.

$$5{,}091{,}867 = 11 \times 462{,}897$$
$$= 9 \times 565{,}763.$$

NOTE. Incidentally, why do we talk about 'factorising' rather than about 'dividing'? Simply because *any* number can be divided by any other number. But when we talk about factorisation we mean finding the two (or more) *whole* numbers that will produce the required result.

For example, the only *factors* of 47 are 47 and 1. But of course you *can* divide 47 by any number you like and get a fractional answer.

AN UNFORTUNATE MUSICIAN

63. The lion who was full of violinist put a paw to his ear and said: 'Eh?'

PALINDROMES

64. If there is anything I like more than anything else it is a problem that is nice and neat. Now look at *this* Palindrome:

WAS IT A CAT I SAW

Nice and neat, don't you think?

ALL ABOARD!

65. Since the two extra passengers would be paying 10s between them, he must have received 10s less than he had contracted for from the others. But the difference between 6s and 5s is 1s. So the original boatload must have been 10, and thus 12 people went on the trip.

KEEPING FIT

66. He must have walked 19 miles the first day, increasing to 25 miles on the last day. We know he covered 164 miles in 7 days, so that his average per day was 22 miles. Since he increased the distance by a mile a day there must have been three days when he did less than 22 miles and three days when he did more. Thus the distance covered on successive days was 19, 20, 21, 22, 23, 24 and 25 miles.

WHAT PRICE ORANGES?

67. The dealer bought his oranges at 9*d* each. Thus he showed a profit of 3*d* on the sale of one orange for a shilling just as he did on selling three for half-a-crown.

But of course his answer was *not* correct. In one case he was getting threepence profit on an outlay of nine-pence (one-third) and in the other case the same profit on an outlay of 2*s* 3*d* (one-ninth). So if it 'didn't matter to him' it ought to have done!

FREQUENCIES

68. Of all the letters in the alphabet the letter E occurs more frequently than any of the others. It is an easy winner, and I expect most of you were able to discover this on your own.

Regarding the remaining 25 letters there are some doubts here, so I will quote from two well-known authorities, and you may find it interesting to compare your own findings with both of these opinions.

Edgar Allan Poe (1809–1849) in his story 'The Gold Bug' (from *Tales of Mystery and Imagination*) gives, after E, the following frequencies of occurrence:

A, O, I, D, H, N, R, S, T, U, Y, C, F, G, L, M, W, B, K, P, Q, X, Z. (He omits J and V.) *It is curious to note that the consecutive letters R, S, T, U appear in the same order in Poe's list.*

In the year 1892, however, a splendid book was published, *Mathematical Recreations and Essays* by W. W. Rouse Ball. This work is still a constant source of reference with problemists and others.

Rouse Ball's order of 'popularity' of letters is as follows:

T, O, A, N, I, R, S, H, D, L, C, F, U, M, P, Y, W, G, B, V, K, X, J, Q, Z.

You will notice quite a number of marked differences between the two lists, in particular the placing of the letter T. I think, however, that Rouse Ball's order is probably the more reliable.

Reverting to Poe, he says in 'The Gold Bug': 'E predominates so remarkably that an individual sentence of any length is rarely seen in which it is not the prevailing character.'

Be that as it may, what was odd about the paragraph I printed as part of the original question?

It does not contain a single E!!

SPOONERISMS

69. A young man took his girl-friend to a dance; and eventually, since it was a lovely, fine evening, they wandered out into the garden and found a seat in a nice secluded spot.

After a few minutes, however, an elderly gentleman, who had been rather overpowered by the heat and the noise in the ballroom, also strolled out into the garden, and chanced to encounter the young man and his girl-friend.

'Ah!', he exclaimed to the young man, 'I see you have found yourself a nosey little cook.'

But you still have to invent some Spoonerisms of your own!

MATCH-STICK WORDS

70. INATTENTIVE, LAMENTATIVE, EFFEM-INATE, TENTATIVE, AFFILIATIVE, TITILLA-TIVE.

By adding 'LY' to any of the above you get two extra letters.

And now, unless you are sick of the subject, you could try the same thing using only curved letters. But I think you will not find anything like as many *long* words because there are only 11 curved letters compared with 15 straight ones. And letters like A, E, I, N, T—all of them 'straight', are extremely useful for a nonsense game like this!

TOO MANY CIGARETTES

71. He needs to buy 343 cigarettes.

When he has smoked them the 343 stubs will make 49 cigarettes, and the stubs of these will make a further 7; and they in turn will make one more.

$$343 + 49 + 7 + 1 = 400.$$

So he will then be left with one cigarette-end to enable him to carry on—the silly fellow!

AN AMAZING WORD SQUARE

72.

R	O	S	E	T	T	E	R
O	V	E	R	R	U	L	E
S	E	Q	U	I	N	E	D
E	R	U	P	T	I	V	E
T	R	I	T	I	C	A	L
T	U	N	I	C	A	T	E
E	L	E	V	A	T	E	S
R	E	D	E	L	E	S	S

JUST SUPPOSING . . .

73. You would save £9,382,499,223,688 10s 7½d. Yes, more than nine billion pounds!

HIDDEN WORDS

74. 1. This letter must BE ANswered quickly. (BEAN)

2. This boy is a little rasCAL, Full of fun.   (CALF)

3. Of the very large meal not a vesTIGE Remains. (TIGER)

4. Living in a monarcHY ENAbles one to pay respect to the CROWn.   (HYENA and CROW)

5. You are such a dreAMER! I CAlled you twice and you took no notice.   (AMERICA)

6. The castle at WindSOR RELies on its visitors' good behaviour.   (SORREL)

MORE HIDDEN WORDS

75. 1. I like watching a fast-flowing river from the towpaTH, RUSHing away to the sea.   (THRUSH and RUSH)

2. When did he GO? O SEven minuteS AGO. (GOOSE and SAGO)

3. Fruit won't ripen on a sunlesS WALL OWing to the coldness of the stone.   (SWALLOW)

4. What is called ofFAL CONsists of heart, liver, KIDneys, etc.   (FALCON and KID)

5. The ice is TOO THin. It should not be walked uPON Yet.   (TOOTH and PONY)

6. A journey to the moon I would caLL A MAd adventure.   (LLAMA)

7. The paSTOR Knows every member of his congregation.   (STORK)

8. Children, you must go to bed—hOW Late it is, MOTHer said.   (OWL and MOTH)

9. For some animals grass is beST, OATs for others. (STOAT)

10. TO ADvertise in the pAPErs costs a lot of money.   (TOAD and APE)

11. What DOEs one find in the ash PAN? THE Remains of the FIRe. (DOE, PANTHER, FIR)

12. The FIRst time I wenT ON ice I hardly dared to move, but with every steP I Grew bolder. (FIR, TON, PIG)

Too easy for you?

JUST IN TIME!

76. When it's 'the eleventh hour'—in the sense of being 'just in time'.

For example, if a train is due to depart at, say, 12.10, and you just manage to catch it with only seconds to spare, you have succeeded at 'the eleventh hour'.

SINGULAR PLURALS

77. (*a*) Buffaloes, (*b*) Calves, (*c*) Duck or ducks, (*d*) Geese, (*e*) Echoes, (*f*) dozen or dozens, (*g*) Gross, (*h*) Taxes, (*i*) Taxis, (*j*) They or them, (*k*) Ourselves, (*l*)There isn't a plural, because there's only one of me! Did you get all of them? I trust so!

ARE YOU RESOURCEFUL?

78. Wrap the end of the string round your first finger, then make a loop around your hand as shown in the illustration.

Now wrap the other end of the string round the other hand, leaving about one foot of string between the two hands.

Clench your hands, bring them together, and then sharply bring your left fist UP and your right fist DOWN. The string will break at the loops in the middle of the palm.

This will work even with the strongest cord!

A CATALYST

79. Just sprinkle a little cigarette ash, or any other ash, on the lump of sugar, and it will immediately catch alight.

IN THE KITCHEN

80. Find a pocket comb, and run it quickly several times through your hair. You have now put a 'static charge' into the comb. (Any bald old gentleman reading this puzzle will have to use somebody else's hair.)

Then hold the comb just above the mixture of salt and pepper—and the grains of pepper, which are lighter than the grains of salt, will jump on to the comb.

AN ANAGRAM

81. MUCH EXTRA LOAD ON BOARD CAN BRING A DEFEAT.

Every letter has been used—and not a single extra one!

RATHER INGENIOUS

82. Naturally the boys on the classical side would know more about Roman numerals than the science boys.

Consequently they quickly realised that the answer must be in Roman numerals. Otherwise the problem is insoluble.

So A = I, B = V, C = X.
And IV multiplied by IV = XVI
Or 4   „   „ 4 = 16.

SOMETHING SIMILAR

83. Here is the key:

100 = C;   500 = D;   50 = L;   5 = V

So we get:

C O D
L I V E R
O I L   *Cod liver oil!*

AND ANOTHER ONE

84.   Turn this book upside down!

DID HE MEET HIMSELF?

85.   Yes, he must at some point on the journey have been at the same place at the same time as he had been the previous day.

Supposing on the second day another man started up the mountain at the identical time, at the same pace, and with the same halts as the first man had used on his upward journey. Clearly at some period or other these two would have to meet, so that at that place and at that particular point of time he would be at the same place as he had been on his outward journey.

Of course we can't be sure at *what* time or at what stage of the trip this would have occurred.

LIGHT-WEIGHT CONTEST

86.   To solve this problem it is first of all necessary to divide the 27 weights into 9 lots of three each, each lot of (ostensibly) the same weight—42 lb. One distribution (I do not claim that it is the only one) is the following: 1, 14, 27; 2, 17, 23; 3, 13, 26; 4, 18, 20; 5, 15, 22; 6, 12, 24; 7, 16, 19; 8, 9, 25; 10, 11, 21.

Weigh any three of these trios against any remaining three; if they balance the light weight is among the untested nine; if one pan of the scale goes down, then the false weight is among those in the other pan.

In any case we have reduced our number of 'doubt-fuls' from 27 to 9. Now of the selected nine weigh one set of three against another, and in the same way the number of 'doubtfuls' will be reduced to three.

Finally, take two of the remaining weights and weigh the heavier against the lighter together with one of the known accurate weights added so as to bring it up to the same apparent weight. The result will enable you to answer the question.

EXAMPLE: Suppose the 17 lb weight to be the light one. Weighing 1, 14, 27, 2, 17, 23, 3, 13, 26 against 4, 18, 20, 5, 15, 22, 6, 12, 24 will show the false weight to be among the first nine. Now weigh 1, 14, 27 against 2, 17, 23, thus finding the false weight to be among the second trio. Now weigh 2 and 15, (the latter known to be accurate) against 17, and it will be seen that the light weight is the 17-pounder. (Of course, if these two had balanced the light one would have been the 23-pounder; if the 17-pounder had been heavier then the false weight would have been the 2-pounder.)

THE CAPITALISTS

87. Suppose John had 2s and Joe 1s. Then one-third of John's money (8d) added to one-quarter of Joe's (3d) would be 11d, and one-quarter of John's (6d) added to one-third of Joe's (4d) would be 10d. But we know the difference was 3d, so each of them must have had three times as much. So John had 6s and Joe had 3s.

IT'S SIMPLY THIS

88. The five sentences are:

1. Is this his?
2. This is his.
3. Is this it?
4. This is it.
5. It is his.

TIME IS MONEY

89. The express train travels 60 miles per hour, whereas the excursion train will take 1½ hours and cost 10*s* less. So he reckons the value of his time at the rate of 10*s* per half-hour or £1 per hour.

SQUARING THE CIRCLE

90. Since the radius of the circle is 1 inch we can omit the 'r' from our calculations and say that the area of the square in square inches should be π, which we know to be approximately equal to 3·1416. (Incidentally, this approximation is sufficiently close to give the circumference of the earth with an error of no more than a fraction of an inch, so that the labour of a mathematician who worked out the values of π to 700 places of decimals was not of much practical value!) So each side of the square must measure $\sqrt{\pi}$ (the square root of π), which works out at about 1·77 inches.

Obviously you cannot measure out 77 hundredths of an inch; your ruler does not mark hundredths of an inch, and if it did you wouldn't be able to see them. Most rulers show divisions of a sixteenth of an inch; you might be able to mark a point midway between two of those divisions, thus giving a thirty-secondth of an inch. If so, mark out a line $1\frac{25}{32}$ inches in length and on it construct your square (that is what you need the compasses for). The area of the square will be $(1\frac{25}{32})^2$ square inches, which works out at about 3·175 square inches—an error of less than one per cent—near enough to accuracy for most purposes.

If you cannot distinguish between thirty-secondths of an inch, then your best effort will be to construct a square with a side of $1\frac{3}{4}$ inches, the area of which will be 3·0625 square inches. Even this is an error of only about $2\frac{1}{2}$ per cent.

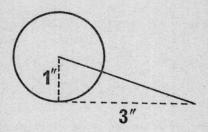

P.S. By the way, if you draw a tangent to your one-inch circle (that is to say at right-angles to the radius) 3 inches in length and join the farthest point to the centre, you will have a line approximating to the length of π inches, with an error of a little over $\frac{1}{2}$ per cent. ($\sqrt{10} = 3\cdot1623$; $\pi = 3\cdot1416$)

REVERSALS

91. The only answer in two digit numbers:

$$13 \times 13 = 169$$
$$31 \times 31 = 961$$

But you can find plenty of larger numbers by inserting noughts. For example:

$$102 \times 102 = 10404$$
$$201 \times 201 = 40401$$

REVERTING TO REVERSALS

92. The smallest number that is a multiple of itself reversed is 8712, which is equal to 2178 multiplied by 4.

The smallest number that is a factor of itself reversed is 1089, which is equal to 9801 divided by 9.

ONE IN NINE

93. Yes, there are several answers. Here are three of them:

173	182	152
295	493	784
468	675	936

Did you find any others?

ONE IN NINE AGAIN

94. Yes, there are *two* answers:

$$
\begin{array}{cc}
192 & 219 \\
384 & 438 \\
\hline
576 & 657 \\
\hline
\end{array}
$$

Maybe there are more than those two solutions—but I shall be very surprised if there are!!

A LITTLE UNUSUAL?

95. The denominator in each case becomes the numerator in the next case. This formula is unique.

JUST A REARRANGEMENT

96. Like this:

```
3 3 3
 333
3 3 3
```

Ingenious, don't you think?

CHINESE IN ONE LESSON

97. Hold the writing up to a mirror!
No, I won't tell you what it says because this requires only a minor effort on your part. Besides which, this is a *serious* book and I don't want to disgrace myself unnecessarily!

A MATHEMATICAL MILKMAN

98. The milkman filled the 3-pint measure, and poured it into the 5-pint measure. Then he again filled the 3-pint measure, and from it completely filled the 5-pint measure.

Now he was left with exactly 1 pint in the 3-pint measure, and thus satisfied his customer's requirements.

OUR MOTHER TONGUE

99. Both sentences are colloquial English, and in each case a preposition has been *permissibly* omitted.

Look at the sentences again with the inclusion of the preposition.

Will you excuse me [for] keeping my hat on?
Will you excuse me [from] taking my hat off.

Another amusing example is in the sentence:

I like nobody's company better than yours.

You will see that this equally means:

1. I like nobody's company more than I like yours.
2. I prefer the company of *nobody* rather than *your* company!

A NICE EASY ONE

100. Waiter, 13*s*; chambermaid, 11*s*; porter, 9*s*; 'boots', 7*s*.

ANOTHER EASY ONE

101.   Smith held 61 cards in his hand.

But perhaps that one was *too* easy. Well, I thought you might want a little rest!

FOR A WET DAY

102.   Sir Samuel Smithers saw sweet Sarah Saunderson swimming. Suddenly she seemed sinking. Sir Samuel stood stunned. Striding seawards, spurning shingle, Sir Samuel swam swiftly Sarahwards. Sir Samuel skilfully supported swooning Sarah; swimming shorewards Sir Samuel successfully succoured Sarah.

Seeming somewhat shaky, Sir Samuel sampled some spirits (special Scotch). Sarah saw Sir Samuel's self-sacrificing spirit. Sir Samuel saw Sarah's sweetness. Sir Samuel soon sought Sarah. Striding slowly Sarah sighed softly, Sir Samuel seemed speechless.

'Say something, Sir Samuel,' said Sarah. 'Say Sam, Sarah', said Sir Samuel. Sarah, smiling shyly, softly said 'Sam'. 'Sarah—Sally', stammered Sir Samuel. 'Sweet Sarah—sweetheart!' Sarah solemnly surrendered.

THIS IS MAGIC

103.   The illustration shows you clearly that the identity of the card is reflected on to the knife.

You must, of course, insert the knife at one of the two *suitable* corners!

SOMETHING IN COMMON

104. Each of the six words contains three consecutive letters in their alphabetical order.

WHERE ARE YOU FROM?

105. (*a*) Aberdonian; (*b*) Liverpudlian; (*c*) Mancunian; (*d*) Glaswegian; (*e*) Novocastrian; (*f*) Orcadian.

P.S. If, however, you happen to come from the village of Little Gidding in Huntingdon I suppose you are a Little Giddinger or Little Giddingite—even if you *aren't* 'Little'. Incidently, T. S. Eliot wrote a poem about the village church. Do you know it?

ANYTHING WRONG HERE?

106.
  1. I am not so tall as he.
  2. *Correct!*

3. *Correct!*
4. Any (or any one) of the three.
5. Let each esteem others as good as himself.
6. *Correct!* (if there are more than two persons. If there are only two then 'They ruined each other' is preferable.)
7. The first two . . .
8. *Correct!*
9. It was unique.
10. I expected to meet you.
11. I should have thought that he would come.
12. We accuse him of . . .

AND AGAIN

107.

1. We acquit him of . . .
2. I ought not to have done it.
3. *Correct!*
4. I am small in comparison with you.
5. *Correct!*
6. *Correct!*
7. I never work when I can avoid it. (No?!)
8. Somehow or other . . .
9. *Correct!* (Also, I am averse *to* that.)
10. Unexceptionable references required.
11. His opinions are approved by all.
12. *Of course it isn't all right! If it weren't raining we could go out and play tennis or something!!!*

WHAT'S THE TIME?

108.   Twenty-five minutes to three.

A FINAL ODD MAN OUT

109.   1. They were all Victorian writers, among whom GEORGE ELIOT was the only woman.

2. They are all animals except LAMA, a Buddhist priest.

3. They are all gods except ISIS, who was a goddess.

SOMETHING WITH MATCHES

110.   Separate the four matches as shown—and you will find your square in the centre.

MATCHES AGAIN

111.   Like this:

If you think this one is unfair, I offer you my apologies!

NEARING THE END

112.   Penultimate—or the last but one.

A KNOTTY PROBLEM

113.   First of all let us have the illustration again, but I have added a few letters and arrows to simplify the explanation.

Make a loop in the string at the point marked A, and pass it through the loop on the wrist at B in the direction of the arrow. Then pass the loop over the hand—and the prisoners will find that they are no longer bound together.

Alternatively the loop at A can be passed through the loop on the wrist at C, and over *that* hand, with the same result. If, however, you make the loop in the other piece of string, you will of course pass it through the loops at D or E. Finally you can join your friends together again by reversing the process.

REMEMBERING NOT TO FORGET

114. Just unfold your arms—and there you are!

ANOTHER KNOTTY PROBLEM

115. The middle one.

A REPETITION

116. The following is the sum in plain figures:

```
        ·  ·
       ·02439
   41)1
      82
      ‾‾
     180
     164
     ‾‾‾
     160
     123
     ‾‾‾
      370
      369
      ‾‾‾
       1
```

Since the first x in the dividend has nothing sub-
tracted from it, and yet leaves no remainder, it is clear
that it must be 1. Also, since *two* figures are brought
down to complete the first division the first figure in the
quotient must be 0; therefore we can represent the
quotient as xxxx (ignoring the 0). Any recurring
decimal is equal to the vulgar fraction represented by
the figures of the recurring decimal divided by 999 . . .
(the same number of 9s as there are figures in the
decimal). So we have $\dfrac{\text{dividend}}{\text{divisor}} = \dfrac{\text{quotient}}{999 \ldots}$, in this case
$\dfrac{1}{xx} = \dfrac{xxxx}{9999}$. The prime factors of 99999 are 3.3.41.271.
Out of these there is only one way of finding a two-
figure number (the divisor), namely 41. Now having
the divisor (41) and the dividend (1), the whole sum
can be reconstructed without difficulty.

Yes? Well, I trust so!

ACROSTICS
AND RIDDLES

ACROSTICS

For those of you who have not hitherto tried to solve
Acrostics, I am first reprinting an example from my
previous book, together with explanations and the
solution.

Down

Right wise, left foolish, people say;
Left's worth a hundred rights today.

Across

1. A vegetable this must be,
   Yet equal cut you seem to see.
2. He asked for more; of tail bereft
   Only a peaceful fruit is left.
3. Fought for the crown, or so we learn.
4. Time to go forward or return.
5. Lydia might be her name
   Or Mrs Mopp—it's all the same.

All the 'Across' clues represent words of which the
first letters and the last ones, if you read them downwards, spell two other words, to which clues are given
in the couplet printed above the other clues.

Take those two downward words first. 'People say'
indicates a proverb or something similar. Can you
think of a popular saying 'something wise, something
foolish'? If not, never mind; we'll go on to the 'across'
words.

Number 1 might be difficult, so we'll skip it for the moment; but surely Number 2 is easy enough. Who was it who 'asked for more'? Oliver Twist, of course. But what about 'of tail bereft'? This must surely mean that you have to knock off the last letter. If you do that with TWIST you are left with TWIS, which doesn't seem very helpful. So try curtailing OLIVER and we are left with OLIVE—clearly a peaceful fruit, since when making up a quarrel we offer the olive branch.

Then Number 3—Who 'fought for the crown?' The lion and the unicorn, of course. For the moment we can't tell which one; but in either case the last letter must be N.

'Time to go forward or return' suggests a word that can be read backwards or forwards; It won't take you long to think of NOON.

So now we have:

```
1. ..........
2. O  liv  E  r
3. ........ N
4. N   oo   N
5. ..........
```

Thus you should be able to guess the uprights: POUND and PENNY (penny wise pound foolish) and a pound is today worth a hundred (new) pennies.

The rest is easy: Number 1 is PARSNIP—a vegetable, and par (equal) snip (cut). Mrs Mopp is the DAILY; and her name, if you change 'daily' around, is Lydia.

That's all there is to it; and the answer is:

P	arsni	P
O	liv	PE r
U	nicor	N
N	oo	N
D	ail	Y

Now you are on your own!

ACROSTICS—No. 1

Down

Pan was his name; a Darling she.
In Neverland they used to be.

Across

1. This playful fight I'm sure you've often tried:
   The prisoner of war gets ill inside.
2. This word is weird and no mistake,
   And headless it would be a lake.
3. Though in a kilt quite often found
   The sailor boy gets nicely browned.
4. Country to which we owe our duty
   Is often found with home and beauty.
5. People like kings and queens may give
   The author wherewithal to live.

ACROSTICS—No. 2

Down

Untested as it, mixed, might well suggest
The greatest of the powers of the West.

Across

1. Set up as only one word, mind:
   A poison tree you'll surely find.
2. Find, when the sun sinks in the west,
   A tangled thing to bring you rest.
3. A lizard, though it seem absurd,
   Has swallowed up a kind of bird.
4. This doctrine quite unchanged is found
   Even if it be turned around.
5. Tax must be paid without a doubt
   Unless, of course, you cut it out!
6. Unhappy man above whose head
   A sword was hanging by a thread.

ACROSTICS—No. 3

Down

Once more astonished? Take a look
Upon the cover of this book.

Across

1. Insurance, this. You might have guessed
   That honesty is far the best.
2. Direction this will indicate;
   To add a ward's unfortunate.
3. A warrior from a distant land,
   His assegai clasped in his hand.
4. A quadruped comes into sight
   Adorned with stripes both black and white.
5. A limb; just add a horn and see
   A well-known town in Italy.

6. Country from which we get some tea;
   Erasers too there well might be.
7. A thin pal, if you mix him well,
   Reveals a tribe of Israel.
8. A joint of ham; but, all the same,
   With back in front you'll find a game.

RIDDLES
(see p. 143)

1. What part of a fish weighs most?

2. Why did the fly fly?

3. Why are clergymen better off than other people?

4. What is it which, though black in itself, enlightens the world?

5. Which of our English monarchs had most reason to complain of his laundry?

6. Why is the Suez Canal like the first 'U' in cucumber?

7. Why is a person who makes bread in want of it himself?

SOLUTIONS TO ACROSTICS

1.   P   illo   W
                  E   eri   E
                  T   arta   N
                  E   nglan D
                  R   oyalt Y

2.   U   pa   S
                  N   igh   T
                  I   guan   A
                  T   ene   T
                  E   xcis   E
                  D   amocle S

3.   P   olic   Y
                  U   nt   O[ward]
                  Z   ul   U
                  Z   ebr   A
                  L   e   G[horn]
                  I   ndi   A
                  N   aphtal   I
           [back]G   ammo   N

CROSSWORD PUZZLES
AND
MORE RIDDLES

A NICE EASY ONE

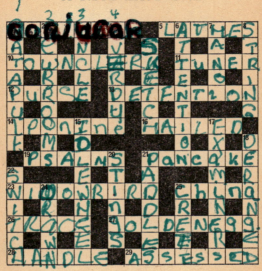

Across

1. Man of magic! (8)
5. Machines that turn and polish. (6)
10. Corporation official. (4, 5)
11. Man for the piano? (5)
12. There might be money in this! (5)
13. Punishment for criminals or schoolboys? (9)
14. Like a lion. (7)
16. Welcomed the downfall? (6)
19. Biblical poems. (6)
21. Dish for Shrove Tuesday. (7)
23. Flying creature in weeds? (5–4)

25. Cups and saucers! (5)
26. Mark of what has been. (5)
27. Once laid by a goose. (6, 3)
28. Move about and manage. (6)
29. Rated. (8)

Down

1. Small boy's weapon? (8)
2. Supposedly they sweep clean. (3, 6)
3. Relative a pawnbroker, perhaps! (5)
4. Not before time! (7)
6. Stand to it! (9)
7. Eastern town in the news. (5)
8. Puppets depend on it. (6)
9. Rough drawing. (6)
15. Lazy circular frame? (4, 5)
17. Trying types! (9)
18. Mad as hatters. (8)
20. Danger from nettles or wasps? (6)
21. Sets foot in the sea. (7)
22. Change the stick. (6)
24. Put in the picture. (5)
25. Re. etc. in the Mediterranean. (5)

RIDDLES
(see p. 143)

8. What musical instrument reminds you of fishing?

9. What colour is grass when covered with snow?

JUST MIDDLING ONES—I

Across

1. Petty thief. (10)
7. At everybody's finger tips. (4)
9. Guitarist's instrument? (7)
10. Blushing colour. (4)
11. Something to crack! (4)
12. Makes for company. (3)
13. Biblical fisherman. (5)
14. Watering place. (3)
15. Before the dawn. (5)
17. Not one's main occupation. (8)
22. Feature of Winter but a spring flower. (8)
25. One kind of ball. (5)

26. Silly creature! (3)
27. Crazy girl? (5)
28. Collegeman. (3)
29. Blow the noise! (4)
32. Industrious scene. (4)
33. Leading lady. (7)
34. Not there! (4)
35. Magnetic charm! (10)

Down

1. One kind of 25 Across. (4, 5)
2. Throw away that piece of steak. (5)
3. Founder of the Police. (4)
4. Famous run. (6)
5. Feeling of well-being. (8)
6. Writing aid in the desk. (3–4)
8. Restrict a junior surgeon! (6)
14. Horse-breeding establishment. (4)
16. Office especially busy at Christmas. (1, 1, 1)
18. 'Odds and ——'. (4)
19. Place of refreshment. (3)
20. Like the holly and the ivy. (9)
21. Chilly cowardly complaint? (4, 4)
23. Simpleton in the soup! (6)
24. They cast spells! (7)
26. Stability for a ship. (6)
30. Excuse—'I wasn't there'. (5)
31. Or little boy by stages. (4)

A RIDDLE
(see p. 143)

10. Why is a billposter the most loyal of servants?

JUST MIDDLING ONES—II

Across

1. Contemporary moulds. (8)
5. Search for them in buildings. (6)
10. Sound invention of Lewis Carroll. (7)
11. Setback in connection with poetry. (7)
12. Towers for Jack? (8)
13. The giddy end! (5)
15. I'd go back first, ram, for the records. (7)
16. Record for a jockey? (4)
19. '—— far away, dissolve & quite forget' (Keats). (4)
21. Little Captain Hornblower? (3, 4)
23. Steal from the smallest. (5)

25. No rave is worth dislike. (8)
27. Nell's fruitful offerings. (7)
28. School of language? (7)
29. Like a certain French Marquis? (6)
30. Descriptive of Hades. (8)

Down

1. Front of a café. (4)
2. Writer under some difficulty, perhaps! (9)
3. I printed adventurously. (8)
4. Needless to say, it's unfinished. (7)
6. Battle against authority. (6)
7. House where beauty may be veiled. (5)
8. Rose-coloured films? (10)
9. Completely blotted out. (6)
14. Society of peculiar people? (10)
17. No place for 7 dn.! (4, 2, 3)
18. Camouflage for the viewer. (8)
20. Sounds like Santa's part of the contract! (6)
21. Shoulder-weapon. (4–3)
22. Amusement grounds? (6)
24. Prize for a minor? (5)
26. In a manner of speaking. (4)

A RIDDLE
(see p. 143)

11. Behead any little thing, and it will become a dangerous weapon. What is it?

NASTY DIFFICULT ONES—I

Across

1. Need for insurance after the second house-warming? (5, 5, 4)
9. They may be hard on unruly schoolchildren! (5)
10. This is not a temporary arrangement. (9)
11. Periodical displays at railway stations. (10)
14. Part of a spicy meat jelly. (5)
16. Farm building in Holland? (5, 4)
18. He plagues people between two hills. (9)
19. Spare part on a set. (5)
20. Perfume from the West Indies. (10)
25. Jewellery depository. (6–3)

26. English malaise in the French town? (5)
27. 'And not by —— —— only (Clough). (7, 7)

Down

2. Swinish writing? (4, 2, 4)
3. Bedroom flowers? (5)
4. Characteristic of the country. (5)
5. Time of grace. (4)
6. Cold comfort in these crevices for climbers. (4)
7. Useful backing for petticoat government? (7, 7)
8. Celestial vegetable? (5, 9)
10. Clapping of hands? (7)
12. Home of so many children! (4)
13. Power used in time of emergency. (7, 3)
15. Ruler in the kitchen. (4)
17. Seated in state. (7)
21. Sparrow's victim. (5)
22. Surrounded by water—must follow? (5)
23. Adversity makes them sweet. (4)
24. Cup-bearer of Olympus. (4)

RIDDLES
(see p. 143)

12. What kind of affection do landlords most appreciate?

13. If a bull went into a draper's shop, what would he require?

NASTY DIFFICULT ONES—II

Across

1. Just a little nip! (8)
5. Sporting music? (6)
9. Inducement to sleep. (8)
10. Lamb-like girl? (6)
11. Departure from Latin. (6)
12. Little publicity in running away. (8)
15. Italian type of panels. (6)
16. Sharp drop! (4)
20. Creatures from Mars. (4)
21. Angler—be it for gain or sport. (6)
25. City of ancient N. Africa. (8)

26. Look at her and turn to stone! (6)
28. Water container not for Eliza's husband! (6)
29. Far-reaching policy. (4–4)
30. Gentle offer. (6)
31. Such a man could stride the world! (8)

Down

 1. Protection against fire. (6)
 2. Man of certain means. (6)
 3. Getting a sun-tan like Robert? (8)
 4. Catch on to some slim girl. (4)
 6. Oppose the fight? (6)
 7. 'H.M.S. ——', ace liner, perhaps! (8)
 8. Wear for widows—in the main? (8)
13. Boil with rage. (6)
14. A watery time of the year? (6)
17. Missile for the wall-game? (7)
18. Greene's was 'Quiet'. (8)
19. A rapid succession of notes. (8)
22. Nourishment for a bowler? (8)
23. Customers or their suppliers. (6)
24. Some cad must have introduced the Greek alphabet. (6)
27. For a game, try looping the loop! (4)

A RIDDLE
(see p. 143)

14. If the Forth Bridge were to collapse, what would they do?
We must hope it won't of course—and I ought to warn you that this is another completely silly one!

SOLUTIONS TO CROSSWORDS

A NICE EASY ONE

JUST MIDDLING ONES

NASTY DIFFICULT ONES

First grid solution (across/down letters):

```
 1T H 2I 3R D P A 4R T 5Y R 6I S 7K
8G   A   O       U   E   C   I
9L I N E S   10P E R M A N E N T
 O   D   E       L   A   R S   C
11B O O K S T A L L S       H
 E   F       U       12S   13M E
14A S P I 15C   16D U 17T C H B A R N
 R   O   H   I   H   O   R   C
18T O R M E N T O R   19E X T R A
 I   K   F   O           I   B
 C       20F 21R A N G 22I P A N I
 H   23U 24H O   E   S   L   N
25O Y S T E R B E D   26L I L L E
 K   E   B   I       E   A   T
27E A S T E R N W I N D O W S
```

Second grid solution:

```
 1F L 2E A 3B I 4T E   5S 6C O 7R E 8S
 E   A   R   W       O   E   E
9N A R C O T I C   10A M E L I A
 D   N   W   G       B   I   W
11E X E U N T   12E 13S C A P A D E
 R   R   I   14S   E   T   N   E
         15N A P L E S   16A C I D
17B   18A   G   R   T   19A   E   S
20R A M S   21F I S H E R
 I   E   22C   N   E   P   23B   24C
25C A R T H A G E   26M E D U S A
 K   I   E       27P   G   Y   D
28B U C K E T   29L O N G T E R M
 A   A   S       L   I   R   U
30T E N D E R   31C O L O S S U S
```

SOLUTIONS TO RIDDLES

1. The scales.

2. Because the spider spider.

3. They always have a surplus (surplice).

4. Ink.

5. King John, when his baggage was lost in the Wash.

6. Because it is between two Cs.
   You could have answered that one yourself if you hadn't looked first!

7. He kneads it.

8. Cast-a-net.

9. Invisible green!

10. Because he always sticks up for his employer.

11. Trifle, rifle.

12. Parental (pay rental).

13. Muslin (Muzzling).

14. Build a fifth!

THE SALVATIONISTS

THE
Salvationists

by
JOHN COUTTS

MOWBRAYS
LONDON AND OXFORD

© The Salvation Army 1977

First published 1977 by
A. R. Mowbray & Co. Ltd.
Saint Thomas House,
Becket St., Oxford OX1 1SJ

ISBN 0 264 66071 4

Printed in Great Britain by
Western Printing Services Ltd, Bristol

Contents

Foreword

This 'survey', *The Salvationists*, is written by one of them; one to whose rich heritage in the Movement has been added distinguished scholarship and a lifelong personal involvement in the work to which all Salvationists are committed.

Agreed the author has not yet met all Salvationists from whom to glean impressions, nor yet encountered all conditions of men among whom Salvationists witness and toil. But where impressions based on actual experience are lacking, insights arising from intuitive perception are not deficient in credibility. What the author has experienced and what he senses combine to provide an illuminating word-picture of the motivation, dedication and infinite variety of those who, in the name and power of Jesus Christ, march under The Salvation Army's banner. If the proper study of The Salvation Army is the Salvationist, all will be exceedingly grateful to John Coutts for the fruits of his research.

July 1977   ARNOLD BROWN
                                                   General

Introduction

Salvationists come in all shapes and sizes. The familiar uniform covers a multitude of personalities, if not of sins. Yet the public at large, when it has no personal knowledge of a Salvationist, regards the Movement with a curiously ambivalent eye. One view is summarized in five words by the children's rhyme:

> Salvation Army
> All gone barmy.

Here the Army is seen as a strange collection of cranks, the religious of the religious, the fringe of a fringe, which condemns the harmless pleasures of the working man. A Scottish newspaper, short of a story, publishes a painting of the Last Supper set in a Glasgow pub. It phones up various churches in search of suitably 'shocked' reactions. Most easily shocked, it seems, are the representatives of the Lord's Day Observance Society and—The Salvation Army. The Army's representative—none other than our friend A Spokesman—would appear to have commented without seeing the picture.

On the other hand there is The Salvation Army that 'does a good work'. After the Aberfan disaster in Wales, in which slag from a disused mine overwhelmed a school, one journalist commented, 'I've made my last joke about The Salvation Army'. He had just interviewed a Salvationist rescuer whose new uniform had been ruined by the mud: all gone barmy perhaps—but for Christ's sake.

Somewhere between the two extremes of Christlike

activism and evangelical oddity the real Salvationists must be found. They are, of course, Christians. Their formal creed proclaims the grand principles of their Methodist forebears; their organization has an autocratic structure unique in Christendom: they are pledged to teetotalism among other things; their officers may only marry other officers; their flag is yellow, red and blue . . . their Movement was founded by William Booth in 1865 . . . Here are a few of them.

ANTHONY is five years old. As a baby he was dedicated under the Salvation Army flag. Now he attends the citadel every Sunday in the large industrial town where he lives. 'Why is our Salvation Army all smashed up?' he asks. He means that the bright electric sign over the door has been shattered by vandals, who have also decorated the outer walls with strange slogans in aerosol paint.

It is hardly surprising that the hall comes under attack. Built in 1909, it used to stand in the heart of working-class housing. The terraced dwellings have now been replaced by high rise flats, but the hall still stands, an architectural relic of a former age, with its foundation stone 'Laid by the Chief Secretary—Hallelujah!' Congregations are smaller than formerly, and the brass band is not very good, but the community is lively, with a number of new young converts.

Anthony likes the Sunday school. He usually loses his attendance card, but he carefully carries home the models and pictures that he produces week by week. How much of the 'story' he grasps is another matter. He likes tales from the Bible—why not?—but he is beginning to be puzzled about death. 'How did Jesus get out from behind that big stone?' he wonders. He says bedtime prayers and thanks God for anything that crosses his mind, calling down blessings on things animate and inanimate, from aunts to fire engines. Since the hall contains no portrait of the bearded Founder, he does not, like some children, confuse God with William Booth.

Anthony's upbringing differs little from that of other children in devout Christian homes. Religion is a natural reality to his parents, and it seems so to him. The time for personal acceptance or rejection lies far in the future—he cannot become a 'Junior Soldier' till he reaches the mystic age of seven. What makes him a 'Salvationist'—if he is one—is the style of the community in which he lives: the absence of tobacco and alcohol, the flag, the plain seats in the hall, the uniforms, the brass band; all these may seem odd to outsiders, but to him they are perfectly natural. On his summer holidays he visited an Anglican church. He was baffled by the choir in their cassocks. 'I didn't like the band in that church', he says. He means the organ.

AFFIONG JOHN is a Nigerian, and a widow. She can read Efik and she speaks a little English. Since she cannot read English her book knowledge is largely limited to the vernacular Bible, of which, like any seventeenth-century puritan, she knows a great deal. Her social life is centred on the local Salvation Army community, and especially its women's organization—the Home League. This meets on Wednesdays at five o'clock in the morning, after which Affiong sets off to the farm. Her work is seasonal, with hard labour in January when the bush is cut down and fired. There is more hard work too at harvest time towards the end of the long rains, when yams and cassava must be harvested and carried home. Affiong's working life often takes her to local markets, and so she has to live in two eccentric cycles: for religion—and most other matters—follows the Western seven-day week, but markets keep to the ancient African eight-day week: so if the village market takes place on Uruaukat-Monday this week, the next one will be on Uruaukat-Tuesday.

Affiong John is a Christian animist—that is to say her world-view is largely pre-scientific. She does not worship the primeval spirits that haunt the river, the stream, the great forest tree; but she believes in their existence, or with part of her mind she believes; and she passes no judgment on her friends who resort, in times of unbearable mental stress, to the help of the ancient gods. But Affiong is out-and-out for the Army, and seeks aid neither of the native doctor's shrine nor of the Christian prophet's prayer house. Nevertheless it is obvious to her, when she dreams of her lost husband, that he is trying to speak to her from the other world. What else could a dream signify? But when she explained this to her only son, to pay whose school fees she works so long and arduously, he—well into physics, chemistry and biology—made fun of the idea: which did not stop her buying him a new blazer, with yellow braid and brass buttons.

She only got angry when her son tried to explain to her how bigoted British missionaries had helped to destroy traditional culture, condemning palm wine and new yam festival and colourful masquerades. What did he know— she asked—about traditional culture? Had he ever seen a suspected wife put to the poison ordeal? Did he know what it was like when the all-male secret societies terror-ized the women of the village, or when girls were put in the fattening house and forbidden to 'learn book'? Affiong can remember from childhood how the Christians marched singing into the forest to cut down the Evil Bush where people abandoned twin babies and smallpox victims and the unhallowed dead. Religion, she says, was hot in those days.

Affiong values her membership of the international Salvation Army. She once helped to present a live sheep to a visiting General; she is working hard with the Home League—both a social service and a kind of Friendly

Society—to raise money for a Maternity Clinic. She has two great worries apart from the endless struggle to find school fees: will her son get a good School Certificate— and will he retain his Christian faith?

HAZEL is 17. Her father and brothers are fishermen. She joined The Salvation Army as a girl of eleven; her friend played in the timbrel brigade and Hazel was fascinated by the music, the rhythm, the endless circles of coloured ribbon. The kindness of the girl who taught her to play the timbrel led her to a personal faith in Christ; an awareness intimate, loyal and unique.

Hazel is general factotum at the local Salvation Army corps. She is Treasurer, Sunday-school teacher, solo soprano and voluntary cleaner. The small community will miss her when she leaves them soon to become Cadet Hazel, embarked on two years' training to become a Salvation Army officer. Hazel has passed her interviews and received her outfit list which contains details of the uniform she has to buy: 'the skirt'—so the instructions tell her—'to touch the floor when kneeling'.

Hazel is going to break with her boy-friend. She is eighteen and he is twenty—an honest unreflective Christian with no bent for heroic sacrifice. She cannot marry him and become an officer, and she knows that if she enters training her chances of finding a husband will be drastically reduced. There is nothing very physical about their relationship: indeed, Hazel, who has read *Sons and Lovers*, has sometimes thought her boy-friend rather slow off the mark—but he has got round to window shopping over furniture and engagement rings. Something has got to be done.

It hurts more than she expected. Hazel has shed the tears of loneliness, walking along the cliff tops above the fishing harbour. She has looked down at the unresting sea and put the question to Christ of whose presence she is among the wheeling seabirds most hauntingly aware. Why does it have to be like this? Why this renunciation? Why now?

Hazel's family are not Salvationists. They pull her leg frequently; they make fun of what they call her frumpish uniform and call her 'Colonel'. When her mother heard that Hazel intended to become an officer, she was bitterly upset. But now, in an odd kind of way, they are extremely proud of her.

JIM is an alcoholic. He was brought up in The Salvation Army and began to play the cornet at the age of seven. By the time he was sixteen Jim was already a solo performer. But then they had a row in the band and Jim left.

One rebel Jew is supposed to have defied his forefathers by standing on a rabbi's grave and eating a ham sandwich. For Jim, raised in a strictly teetotal environment, a half-pint seemed as good a weapon as any in the war of independence. He became a wandering boy far gone in the ways of sin: that is to say, he smoked, drank, and played darts in pubs. But a fate almost worse than death awaited him.

The frightful cycle of alcoholism broke Jim's marriage and cost him several jobs. He had married an attractive girl, and as he watched the lines of mental pain grow ever tighter on her face, he knew full well who was responsible for them. At last Jim came to share the subculture of the alcoholic vagrant, a world almost as remote from suburban man as that of the hedgehog and the fieldmouse; following strange paths, sleeping in strange places, eating strange food or no food at all.

Yet Jim has never ceased to believe in God. Theologians of an earlier generation would have debated earnestly as to whether Jim's belief added up to 'saving faith' or not. It must have added up to something, for Jim, in and out of prison, much counselled by Alcoholics Anonymous, finds himself once more at the Penitent-form.

Jim's penitence is real; his tears sincere. He has already gone for six months without a slip. He has phoned his wife—not to ask for a new start, but only to tell her that he is trying again. The Captain is trying to find him digs and a job.

The Captain also wonders whether he should talk to Jim about becoming a committed Salvationist. He was taken 'off the roll' years ago, and has lost a crucial document that he signed as a teenager without taking it very seriously: Salvationists call it the *Articles of War*. We shall find out more of this in the next chapter.

PART ONE

WHAT THEY BELIEVE

The Creed they Profess

On the first Sunday evening of 1976, The Salvation Army citadel at Ilford in East London is fairly full. The congregation occupies the ground floor and fills several rows of the large overhanging gallery. The band sits on the platform, about thirty strong. In front of them, and facing the congregation, are the Captain and his wife. They are flanked, as ancient custom requires, by the Secretary, Treasurer, and Sergeant Major—the senior 'laymen' of the corps. Before worship begins there is a notable absence of holy hush—or indeed of hush of any kind. The meeting gets off to a good start with an old gospel song 'Whosoever heareth, shout, shout the sound'. Then follows prayer by the Captain, and the reading of a suitable Bible portion—it comes in fact from the second book of Chronicles. Then the band plays a piece entitled 'Constant Trust': in essence a weaving together of familiar gospel hymns and choruses. This, we are told, is offered as a tribute to one of its most loyal members, who died in his car, having locked up after the youth club a few days before. The Captain may well wonder, as he surveys the scene, whether the youth club will now fold up for lack of leaders; but at least there are compensations, for after the band has played we come to the heart of today's matter— the enrolment of six new salvation soldiers.

Over the centuries Christians have developed many and various rites of initiation. Some have been baptized in rivers, and others in tanks at the back of chapels. Some have been sprinkled and others immersed. To some the right hand of fellowship has been offered. On others the hands of bishops have been laid. The ceremony of the swearing-in of Salvation Army soldiers is a curiously formal ritual for a Movement which claims earnestly that rituals avail a man nothing at all.

One young man, two women and three teenage girls are called to stand on the platform beneath the Army's yellow, red and blue flag. Only one has so far bought the familiar navy-blue uniform. Standing on either side of the Captain, the six—who include a mother and her daughter—pledge allegiance to God in terms of the promises they have made in a document called the *Articles of War*. After prayer, the new comrades are welcomed 'in the old style' with a round of applause, and the Captain draws our attention to the fact that the *Articles of War*—venerable document—have now appeared in a new format. The illuminated copy no longer contains those illustrated cameos of missionaries in far-flung lands. But if the picture has changed, the prolix wording is identical with that of 1882.

In Britain in the 1970s, the swearing-in of new soldiers is not as common a ceremony as it used to be. The average increase per congregation in England and Wales is only 2·03, a figure well below the wastage brought about by death and indifference. But the six recruits have made up their minds in genuine liberty. They may not be thrown to the lions, but neither are they signing on for profit. Social currents run in the opposite direction.

So to the *Articles of War*: 'Having received with all my heart the salvation offered to me by the tender mercy of God, I do here and now acknowledge God the Father to be my King; God the Son, Jesus Christ our Lord, to be my Saviour; and God the Holy Spirit to be my Guide, Comforter and Strength, and I will, by His help, love, serve, worship and obey this glorious God through time and in eternity.'

So this is the vow of a salvation soldier. . . . No, it appears to be only the first paragraph. The six recruits are now called on to assent to 'the truth of the Army's teaching, that is to say. . .'.

There follow 11 articles of faith—28 less than the total professed, for example, by the Church of England, but quite enough to discourage anyone who thinks a prospective Salvationist commits himself only to creedless benevolence.

In Henry Fielding's *Tom Jones*, the energetic Parson Thwackum declares: 'When I mean religion I mean the Christian religion, and not only the Christian religion but the Protestant religion, and not only the Protestant religion but the Church of England.' The Army's creed likewise proclaims a version of Christianity Western, not Eastern, Protestant not Roman Catholic, and Methodist not Calvinist. Indeed the 11 articles are Methodism of the purest vintage, for the pioneers who rallied to William Booth in East London in the 1860s were nearly all Methodists.

When, in 1878, the Christian Mission turned into The Salvation Army, William Booth made haste to assure readers of the Movement's magazine that nothing had changed but the name. 'We believe in the old-fashioned Salvation. We have not developed or improved into Universalism, Unitarianism, or Nothingarianism, and we don't expect to. Ours is just the same Salvation taught in the Bible, preached by Luther and Wesley and Whitfield . . . purchased by the agony and sufferings and blood of the Son of God.'

The faith taught in the Bible had already been expressed first in 7 and then in 11 articles of belief—the same that were assented to by our six recruits in 1976. They affirm that the Bible is the inspired word of God, that there is only one true God who exists in Trinity, that Christ is both God and Man, that man is a sinner exposed to God's wrath, that salvation comes by repentance and faith, that Christ has made an atonement for the whole world, that believers may, if unfaithful, fall from grace and be lost, that they may, on the other hand, live lives holy and blameless before God; that the soul is immortal and that endless happiness awaits the righteous and endless punishment the wicked.

William Booth was not quite accurate in saying that the Movement's message was the same gospel as was preached by Wesley and Whitfield. For on several key issues he took sides with the former against the latter. A century before, the old mystery of predestination had divided the ranks of the saints. Whitfield had followed John Calvin and opted for the doctrine of predestination. Since God is all-powerful He must have foreordained, from all eternity, that some—the elect—shall be saved, and others—the reprobate—shall be lost. Hence it follows that Christ died for the elect only, and not for all, that God's grace must be irresistible, and that a believer, once converted, can never totally fall away from grace. Against these iron doctrines the Methodists, in agreement with the Dutchman, Arminius, had maintained that God had foreknowledge of those who would be saved, but that He did not overrule man's freewill. Christ therefore died for all, not for the elect; and a believer, possessing freewill, could, after conversion, fall away and be lost. Controversy on these points was so hot in the eighteenth century that Wesley said to the Calvinist Whitfield: 'Your God is my devil.'

Nor had the old fires ceased to burn in 1851, when the future General Booth applied for training at Cotton End Congregational Academy, near Bedford—but then withdrew: 'Disapproving of the manner in which the committee had conducted his examination on the disputed doctrines of Arminianism.'

Thus, if the pioneer Salvationists were not Universalists, Unitarians, or Nothingarians, they were not Calvinists either. In 1873 the Conference of the Christian Mission directed an anathema against those who denied freewill: 'Resolved that no person shall be allowed to teach . . . the doctrine of final perseverance . . . if any such person after having been cautioned by the Superintendent continued to teach this doctrine, they should not be allowed further to preach or speak in the mission.'

Our six recruits, we may be almost sure, are unaware of the battles fought long ago on the question of the 'Final Perseverance of the Saints'. Nor will they have realized that the tenth article of faith to which they have assented was intended to assert the full Methodist doctrine of entire sanctification. In 1876 George Scott Railton, prophet and eccentric, added a rider to the effect that 'after conversion there remain in the heart of the believer inclinations to evil, or roots of bitterness . . . these evil tendencies can be entirely taken away by the Spirit of God . . . and the whole heart . . . will then produce the fruit of the Spirit only'.

Poor Railton—his sons bitterly disappointed him by going to Oxford and joining the Church of England—was convinced that the Methodists were losing the fire as the Quakers had done before them. He and the other missioners wanted their faith to express those insights into Christian truth which, they thought, would keep the blaze going permanently.

For creeds are like ancient and abandoned fortifications, monuments to intellectual conflicts of a bygone age. Why, asks a heedless and indifferent generation, did they spill ink or blood for this? Even the devout Christian of the twentieth century would find it hard to explain the young William Booth's dispute with the trustees at Cotton End. In 1851 people were still arguing as to whether Christ died for all, or only for some, yet in 1846 George Eliot—a Christian no longer—published her translation of the *Life of Jesus* by David Strauss. Its readers might well wonder whether Christ had ever lived, let alone died, at all. In 1859 *The Origin of Species* was published, and six years later T. H. Huxley, soon to be one of the Army's bitterest critics, defended Darwin against Bishop Wilberforce in the famous 'ape or angel' controversy. The East London Christian Mission got going in 1865—a year after Karl Marx had published the first volume of *Das Kapital*, proposing quite different solutions to the problems of the working man. The Mission became The Salvation Army in 1878, and two years later the atheist Charles Bradlaugh —a man in temperament and character remarkably similar to William Booth—was excluded from the British Parliament for refusing to swear by almighty God. Occasionally, the missioners would clash with 'Bradlaugh's atheist crew' in the East End. But what of the battle for the mind? The Salvation Army came into existence, with a creed restating the classic doctrines of evangelical Protestantism, at the very moment when the foundation of that faith appeared to be shaken. The infallible Bible, the creation of man by God in the Garden of Eden . . . were not the Nothingarians thundering at the gates, or perhaps we ought to say, gnawing away at the foundations?

Consider the chief corner-stone of the system—the inspiration of the Bible. When the pioneers asserted that 'the Scriptures of the Old and New Testaments were given by inspiration of God', they meant, no doubt, to assert the traditional Christian doctrine of a totally reliable Bible, graciously given by God and free from mistakes. They saw no need to define the matter further, and to assert that the Bible was 'inerrant' or 'verbally inspired'. This was just as well, for they left room— perhaps unwittingly—for 'liberals' and 'conservatives', 'fundamentalists' and 'modernists', to coexist, at times uneasily, in the Army of the future. Thus William Robertson Smith, on trial before the General Assembly of the Free Church of Scotland for his 'higher critical' views on the Bible in 1876–80, was able to claim that he accepted the classic Westminster Confession with all his heart. Nor was this surprising. The fathers and brethren who drew up that document in the seventeenth century had never condemned the Higher Critics—for the latter did not exist in their day!

But Robertson Smith and his like got short shrift from the Army Mother, Catherine Booth. Speaking in Princes Hall, Piccadilly in 1886, she condemned: 'Christian free-thinkers' who 'deny whatever seems to them to be objectionable in the Scriptures. The inspiration of the Bible is to them on a level with that of Homer or Shake-speare, and for anything they do not like they have a free rendering, or a cool excision. They . . . take away what they fancy to be stumbling-blocks in the path of men . . . the law which is to train servants for the eternal household of the King of kings . . . may be treated with a free hand . . . according to the notions of men who love their own will better than anything else in heaven and earth.'

So there were no 'Christian freethinkers' in the Army's ranks—or were there? If so, when and where did they first appear?

Among the Primitive Methodists—first cousins to the Army—the scholar A. S. Peake brought out his influential 'liberal' commentary in 1919. No doubt subterranean streams of thought were flowing in the Army too, but to trace their course is far from easy. In 1910 A. M. Nicol, the Army's erstwhile editor-in-chief, declared that some of his former colleagues did not take the old 'Methodistic articles' seriously. Who? How? Since when? Nicol, alas, did not say.

The fact is that the Army's military constitution gives the Movement the appearance of a monolith. No general assembly meets year by year. The administration controls the press, which rarely airs controversial issues, and certainly not if these touch the life of the Army itself. The would-be officer does not have a choice of Colleges— liberal and conservative—to suit his own opinions. Thus one looks in vain for open play on the intellectual field. The ball remains obscurely in the scrum, and spectators can see little of what is going on, though now and again players are injured, and very occasionally sent off the field.

By 1905 officers who followed the Army's Bible correspondence course were dealing with Genesis and geology. 'The chronology of the Bible', they were told, 'is a million-fold more reliable than the dates, if such they can be called, which most astronomers and geologists use.' And in dealing with difficulties over Noah's flood, students were advised to follow the guidance of 'one great and devout Scotsman, who has since gone to his reward'. This scholar—not Robertson Smith, presumably —held that you could find no traces of Noah's flood because the Lord had removed them on purpose.

But this splendid explanation cannot have satisfied everybody, for in 1905 Bramwell Booth published an article entitled *The Salvation Army and the Higher Criticism*. 'Mr Bramwell'—William Booth's eldest son— was Chief of the Staff and already the power behind the throne, if not yet on it. Noting that 'a number of Church of England ministers have recently signed a document asking for greater freedom to question some of the truths usually accepted by Christians', Bramwell proceeded to point out that 'Higher Critics' were far from unanimous themselves. So were the 'Christian freethinkers' in for another lambasting? Would the traditional view of the Bible be restated? It might look like it, but in fact Bramwell was laying down a heavy barrage to cover his troops while he marched them into new positions.

'It has always been my view', he declared, 'that the Bible must be treated as a whole, and that we cannot abandon the outposts . . . without imperilling the citadel. Any attack on the Old Testament . . . no matter how pious its authors, is in reality a challenging of the knowledge or the sincerity, and therefore of the divinity of Jesus Christ Himself.'

This looks like the classic conservative argument. Did Moses write the Book of Exodus, for example? Higher Critics say no—but Jesus says yes (Mark 12.26). And Jesus must be right, for He is the Son of God.*

But how do we know that Jesus is the Son of God? Surely because the Bible says so—and the reliability of the Bible is the very point in question! Bramwell Booth breaks out of the circular argument by appealing to experience. 'We say not that the revelation of Christ to the soul depends on the truth of the Bible, thus leaving us at the mercy of every storm of criticism that assails its records . . . the truth of the Bible is established by revelation of Jesus Christ in us and the glorious fulfilment in our hearts and lives of just precisely what it promises.'

In other words, whereas classical Protestantism held that the Bible guaranteed the truth about Jesus, Bramwell argues that our experience of the love of Jesus guarantees the truth of the Bible. Did the readers of *The Field Officer* —the article was not made available to the rank and file—

---

* Could Jesus, though Son of God, have limited knowledge? Bramwell does not seem to consider this idea.

notice where the Chief of the Staff was taking them? Other regiments in the Lord's army were executing similar manoeuvres. To quote Rupert E. Davies: 'During the second half of the nineteenth century . . . people sensed . . . that the Bible was under fire . . . long before they seriously studied the attacks of the critics. But the Bible was the source of their doctrine. What were they to do if the Bible was taken from them? The best thing . . . was to fall back on experience, which biblical criticism could not touch, and so experience gradually took over the place of the Bible as the source of doctrine' (*Methodism*, p. 98).

Bramwell Booth seems to have followed a similar technique in dealing with the theory of evolution. In an interview entitled 'Man, monkey and moonshine' (*War Cry*, 10 September 1927) he took aim at Sir Arthur Keith, President of the British Association, for saying that Charles Darwin was probably right and that man had evolved from a lower species. 'We stand by the Bible . . .' declared the General: 'Any suggestion that . . . Jesus Christ died for a race of anthropoid apes is utterly repulsive.'

What could be clearer than that? Yet the questioner went on to ask '. . . you would not have in the Army a man, who though he were to come to the Penitent-form, yet thought as did some of these Darwinian folks?'

'I never said that', was the reply, 'nor did the Founder. A man may have ever such mistaken views, but as long as he believes in Jesus Christ . . . and is ready to fight for souls . . . he may come under my umbrella.' The man would apparently soon see the error of his ways.

But what if he persisted in them? Might not a Darwinian recruit develop into a Darwinian soldier, Captain, Colonel, General? Certainly it was clear, by the late 1920s, that some Salvationists at least had come to terms with the theory of evolution, and meanwhile were making up their own minds about the inspiration of the Bible too. In 1927 A. G. Cunningham, a Commissioner and a leading intellectual whose thinking lay behind the 1923 *Handbook of Doctrine*, published a paper in which, clearly and explicitly, the idea of an infallible Bible was abandoned. Once more, devout Scotsmen offered their help: 'The Bible, is in the first instance, a means of grace. . . . Dr James Orr, a stout opponent of extreme criticism, has declared "the fact that the Bible has this gospel at the heart of it . . . proves that it is God's word. The evangelists may make mistakes in dates and in order of events, in reporting the occasion of a word of Jesus . . . even though on a number of occasions of this kind the Gospels should be proved to be in error, the GOSPEL is untouched; the word of God, the revelation of God to the soul in Christ, lives and abides".'

In other words, the Bible is inspired, because it is inspiring. Cunningham ended with a quotation from yet another devout Scotsman. 'If I am asked why I receive the Scriptures as the word of God . . . I answer . . . because in the Bible alone I find God drawing nearer to man in Christ Jesus and declaring to us in Him His will for our salvation. And this record I know to be true by the witness of the Spirit in my heart. . . .'

And which devout Scotsman said that? None other than Robertson Smith at his trial for heresy in the 1880s! The 'Christian freethinker' was now welcomed as an ally. Liberal attitudes to the Bible were now at home in The Salvation Army.

Or were they? Cunningham's articles appeared in 1927 in the *Staff Review*, a journal restricted to Lieutenant-Colonels and above. They were not made available to the rank and file in book form till 1961. Thus obscurely, imperceptibly, does the scrum struggle down the field.

For the process of rethinking took place not only within the Army, but in every church, and in the mind of every Christian who thought seriously about his faith at all. Furthermore the attitudes of Salvationists were conditioned more by the thinking and scholarship of those outside the Army than by those within. And in North America the gulf between 'liberal' and 'conservative' attitudes to scripture was much wider than in Britain. From 1910 onwards in the United States a series of pamphlets entitled 'The Fundamentals' defended such traditional beliefs as an infallible Bible, and the 'penal substitution' theory of the atonement. Hence the not very helpful labels 'fundamentalist' and 'modernist' attached to the contending parties. Both schools of thought are represented throughout the Army world, but theological attitudes have remained much more conservative in the United States than in Britain. Thus, for example, the *Manual of Salvationism*, approved for the training of recruits in the United States, comes out plainly for the *verbal inspiration* of the Bible. 'Holy Men were fitted and guided by the Holy Spirit to receive and record *truth* as revealed to them by God . . . both the Bible writers and the Bible itself are "God-breathed" or inspired. Consequently the Book comes to us with divine authority and trustworthiness. It does not only *contain* the word of God, but it *is* the word of God.'

So why all the fuss from biblical critics? 'Certain alleged errors and discrepancies', says the *Manual*, 'often only appear to be such, and are all of minor importance.'

Thus The Salvation Army, like many other Christian bodies, is deeply divided over its attitude to Scripture. Yet there has never been an open schism on the issue, and Salvation Army unity and comradeship have not been affected. This could be in part because every territory has its quota of liberals and conservatives and partly because the Movement's military constitution keeps the fires of controversy well and truly damped.

One might indeed argue that the Army's progress in an increasingly secular world is a tribute to the vitality of its message. T. H. Huxley, champion of Charles Darwin and inventor of the term 'agnostic'—was bitterly hostile. 'Few social evils', he wrote of the Army in 1891, 'are of greater magnitude than unobstructed and unchastened religious fanaticism.' Friedrich Engels, the pioneer Communist, took a kinder view. The Army, he declared, 'revives the propaganda of early Christianity, appeals to the poor as to the elect, fights capitalism in a religious way, and thus fosters an element of early Christian class antagonism which may one day become troublesome to the well-to-do people who find the money for it'. He paused for a side-swipe at Huxley and agnosticism which 'though not yet considered "the thing" quite as much as the Church of England, . . . decidedly ranks above The Salvation Army.'

But Engels' hopes, and Huxley's fears of a revolutionary socialist army were both due for disappointment. Religion has remained the Army's business.

A subtler foe was Sigmund Freud. As Bramwell Booth —like many another Christian thinker—was rallying his troops on the unshakeable ground of personal religious experience, Freud proceeded to argue that religious experience was in fact illusion. Yet there was need for a band of dedicated spirits to work as lay assistants in the war against mental pain and neurosis: 'A new kind of Salvation Army', said Freud (The question of lay analysis in *Two Short Accounts of Psycho-analysis*, p. 170) could help his work. Clearly he respected the motives, but not the message, of the old one.

For that message has remained religious. The 'Nothing-arians' have not yet taken over. The Army as a whole has continued to profess a Christ-centred, devout and personal

faith. Yet in spite of William Booth's prophecy of 1878,
the Universalists seem to have gained ground in its ranks,
at any rate in the Western world. The old concern with
the next world, and especially with hell, has largely disappeared. In the late 1920s articles can be found in the
files of the London *War Cry*, written by such theological
heavy-weights as Samuel Brengle, upholding the importance of the preaching of hell. We may deduce that
there were doubters, who did not publish articles. At the
same time the number of hymns about hell declines from
edition to edition of the Army's song book. Who still sings

> What scenes of horror and of dread
> Await the sinner's dying bed
> Death's terrors all appear in sight,
> Forerunners of eternal night. . . ?

For nowadays, in the West at least, the nurse with the
painkilling injection appears for both sinner and saint
alike.

Eternal death disappeared altogether from the young
people's song book published in 1963, which includes a
section on 'heaven' but not about the other place. Hell,
it would seem, is now for adults only.

Here is a shift of emphasis that has occurred in all the
Western churches. . . . And yet if continued 'singability'
is a good test of theological truth, then it would seem that
the great positive affirmations of the pioneer Salvationists
are as valid as ever. After the recruits have made their
promise there is no difficulty about the Founder's song:

> O boundless salvation, deep ocean of love,
> O fullness of mercy, Christ brought from above,
> The whole world redeeming, so rich and so free,
> Now flowing for all men, come roll over me.

For when William Booth contended for the idea that

Christ died for all, and not only for the elect, he was moved more by pity for the Nottingham poor than by intellectual dislike of Calvinism. Creeds are not wholly negative things. Too often aimed merely at getting heretics out, they also serve—at least partially—to convey what the Christian community holds dear. And to assert the infinity of God's love for the undernourished child, the muddled alcoholic, the ordinary man in the street, remains at the heart of The Salvation Army's teaching. Our new soldiers are not likely to have heard of John Smith, the Cambridge Platonist of the seventeenth century, but they might well find him expressing their own deepest feelings: 'It is but a thin airy knowledge that is got by mere speculation . . . that which springs forth from true goodness . . . is more clear and convincing, than any demonstration . . . were I indeed to define divinity, I should rather call it a divine life, than a divine science, it being something rather to be understood by spiritual sensation, than by a verbal description.'

This it is with Salvationist as with all true Christian theology. Articles of Faith are but dry bones, unless they are clothed in the living flesh of inward perception and active love. But they certainly form part of the inheritance of those new salvation soldiers being sworn-in on that Sunday evening at Ilford Citadel. And the *Articles of War*, which make profound affirmations about God, also claim that The Salvation Army is 'raised up, directed and sustained by' Him. The Army, in other words, is part of the Church of Christ. But does it, by itself, constitute a 'church'. And if not, then what is it?

The Army and the Churches

In the minds of our recruits, the step they are taking probably corresponds to being confirmed in the Church of England, or baptized in the Baptist Chapel. Yet the *Articles of War*, apart from claiming that God raised up the Army, say nothing about other denominations at all. Did the Lord likewise raise up the Lutherans, the Methodists, the Mormons, the Jehovah's Witnesses. . . ? One need feel no surprise, however, if the early Salvationists had little interest in theorizing about the Church catholic. The first generation of Christians had little interest in it either. A new movement is more concerned with getting on with the job than with defining rules of membership, ousting dissidents and setting up archives. Theorizing about the constitution can be left to the third and fourth generation.

Three views about the Church have been distinguished down the centuries. First of all there is the hierarchical view. Here, as J. S. Whale wrote: 'There is a visible . . . institution, which is the divinely commissioned vehicle and guarantee of the truth and the grace of the gospel.' The Roman Catholic Church is the largest but by no means the only denomination of this kind.

Secondly we have the classical Protestant view of the Church, as expressed, for example, by the Scottish covenanters in the seventeenth century. Here the Church is founded on the word of God, with faithful preaching, a duly constituted ministry and right administration of the sacraments. Here there is no 'pipeline' of bishops stretching back to the apostles, but instead an organization, which in the days of its power, could be as oppressively clerical as anything achieved by the old religion.

And so to the third component of Christian awareness: if Rome exalts tradition, and Geneva cries up the Bible, the radical wing of the Reformation emphasizes the sovereignty of the Holy Spirit. 'The Lord opened unto me', declared George Fox, 'that being bred at Oxford and Cambridge was not enough to fit and qualify men to be ministers of Christ.' The Founder of the Quakers perceived that 'this struck at Priest Stevens' ministry'. 'I would get into the orchards and the fields with my Bible, by myself', he declared, concluding that his own task was to 'bring people off from Jewish ceremonies, from heathenish fables, and from men's inventions', to realize 'God's unspeakable love for the world.'

And in 1881 George Scott Railton, General Secretary of the Christian Mission and first Salvation Army Commissioner, produced a pamphlet about the redoubtable Quaker, using as frontispiece an engraving of Fox interrupting a sermon by the parish priest of Ulverstone. 'Whatever would they say if the Army did this?' asked Railton, making his parallel even plainer with another picture showing seventeenth-century hooligans 'mobbing and beating The Salvation Army of 1652'.

Radical Christian groups, such as stemmed from the 'left wing' of the Reformation, have naturally emphasized the sovereignty of the Holy Spirit and tended towards independency and democracy in Church government. . . . If the Spirit is poured out on all believers, then surely authority must reside, not in bishop or minister, but in the church meeting gathered to ascertain the Spirit's will? And here the paradox of The Salvation Army's structure becomes apparent at once: a group whose theology professes salvation through faith alone, and declares that no priest can come between a man and his Maker, that no outward rite or sacrament can avail—has developed an organization which an unfriendly critic sees as 'a poor and profane imitation of the faith and authority of the church of Rome'.

There were many cross-currents in the evangelical movement in nineteenth-century Britain. The 'old dissenters' (Baptists, Presbyterians, Congregationalists, Quakers) who had parted company from the Established Church in the seventeenth century, had been reawakened by the appearance of Methodism in the eighteenth. Led with zeal and authority by John Wesley, the Methodists felt driven, step by step, to part company with the Church of England. The decisive break came in 1784, when Wesley, frustrated by the refusal of the Anglican bishops to provide spiritual care for Methodists in North America, decided to do so himself. But Thomas Coke, the American 'Superintendent', had ideas of his own. Across the ocean superintendents became bishops, and the American Methodist Episcopal Church was born.

Meanwhile, back in Britain, the Methodist movement had its ups and downs. The constitution bequeathed by John Wesley was far from democratic, and the Wesleyans were felt to be too conservative, both in religion and politics. Thus the New Connexion—of which the young William Booth was ordained a minister—was set up in 1797. Next Hugh Bourne, influenced by the success of the great 'camp meetings' that were taking place among the frontier folk in America, held the first British camp meeting on Mow Cop in Staffordshire in 1805. Orgies were suspected, both sexual and political. Bourne was expelled by the Wesleyans in 1808, and the Primitive Methodists came into being in 1810. In the West of

England the freelance efforts of William O'Bryan led to
the establishment of the Bible Christian societies in 1815.
Among the Bible Christians appear several features that
would be typical of the future Salvation Army. If O'Bryan
could not make himself General it was not for want of
trying. 'The Bible Christian conference', writes Rupert E.
Davies, 'resisted his claim to be a perpetual President and
decide all matters by his single vote, and he set off to
found a new sect in America and Canada.' The Bible
Christians too, were the first to allow itinerant women
preachers—'whom the men preachers were connexionally
advised to marry'. In The Salvation Army the rule that an
officer may marry only another officer still prevails. Moreover, Billy Bray, 'the King's son', converted among the
Bible Christians, sounds like one of the Salvationist
'trophies' of a generation later. 'I can't help praising the
Lord. As I go along the street I lift up one foot, and it
seems to say "glory", and I lift up the other, and it seems
to say "Amen".'

In William Booth's personal career the movement of
English Church history repeated itself: baptized in the
Church of England, he grew up among the Wesleyan
Methodists. Ordained in the New Connexion, he resigned
in 1859 because he was not allowed to work full time as a
travelling evangelist. Finally he became the founder of a
new denomination, while believing—like most founders of
denominations—that he was doing nothing of the kind.

The constitution of the East London Christian Mission
in its early years closely resembled that of the various
Methodist denominations from which so many members
had come. Government was by Annual Conference,
although the General Superintendent—William Booth—
was a permanent fixture. Women were admitted to the
government of the mission as well as to membership,
and total abstinence from alcohol was required for all

office bearers, but not as yet for members as well.

Yet it might have been suspected that the Annual
Conference would not last long. A Deed Poll of 1875
declared that the 'Christian Mission is and shall be hereafter for ever under the oversight, direction and control
of one person'. The one person—William Booth—had
power to nominate his successor and to veto conference
decisions. How long would it be before the General
Superintendent—already known as 'The General' for
short—would suspend the constitution and rule by decree?

Yet the Annual Conference was never turned out of
doors. 'By the year 1876', wrote the Mission's secretary,
George Scott Railton, 'it had become evident that the
speed of the mission's advance must make the resolutions
of an annual conference comparatively useless.' The last
conference of 1878 was the first War Congress of The
Salvation Army. Railton admitted that 'some old heads
were shaken and possibly some true hearts were saddened',
but in a Movement that was doubling in size each year,
the old heads could not muster enough votes to stop the
Annual Conference putting an end to itself. Evangelists
would no longer be stationed by committee, but by
William Booth. 'This is a question of confidence', he had
declared in 1877. 'Confidence in God and in me are
absolutely indispensable both now and ever afterwards.'

The deed poll of 1878 replaced that of 1875, making
William Booth General Superintendent for life, with power
to nominate his successor, as well as sole trustee. Absolute
monarchy had arrived.

And so too had the new name. The printer's proof of
the Mission's report for 1878 declared:

THE CHRISTIAN MISSION

IS . . .

A VOLUNTEER ARMY

An explanatory quotation from Archbishop Tait of Canterbury declared: 'We welcome every volunteer who is willing to assist the regular forces . . . arm . . . the whole population in the cause of Jesus Christ.' But the 'volunteers' were the Home Guard—the 'Dad's Army'—of the day, and the corrected proof declared:

THE CHRISTIAN MISSION

IS . . .

A SALVATION ARMY

The new name fitted the new constitution. Railton was well satisfied. 'We have got an organization managed upon the simple business-like principles of a railway, with all the cohesion and co-operative force of a trade union, formed of people whose devotion, determination and confidence at least equal that of the Jesuits . . . all of whom are left to enjoy and use . . . perfect spiritual freedom and independence. . . .'

Ironically, a major victim of the new railway type constitution would be Railton himself, whose mercurial gifts did not fit in with the new system. Fearing that the Movement was departing from purely spiritual ideals, he burned his boats in 1894, by appearing in sackcloth at the Queen's Hall and solemnly trampling underfoot an advertisement for the new Salvation Army Assurance Society.

'The constitution of the Army is so dogmatic and binding for all time that if at any period . . . a number of its leaders were to petition for the right to elect the General by ballot . . . the General for the time being would have no power to grant such a petition.'

Such was the prophecy of A. M. Nicol in 1910. He was wrong, but his insight foreshadowed personal tragedy and constitutional crisis.

For absolute autocracy had already been modified in

1904. The aged William Booth had been advised to do something about the constitution by various worthies from Mr Gladstone down. He therefore executed a supplementary deed poll, allowing for the summoning of a High Council and the removal from office of an insane, unfit, or criminal General. The document was prepared by the Founder's son, Bramwell Booth, who was later to be himself the first—and so far the only—General to be deposed under its provisions.

For the system whereby the General remained sole trustee and had power to nominate his successor simply could not last. The second generation of Booths were divided by it. In 1902 Herbert Booth resigned—in Australia—calling for 'a government . . . in which . . . leading spirits throughout the world shall have a voice. . .'. In 1904 Maud and Ballington Booth left the Army to found the Volunteers of America. Two years later the Army in the United States—which retained most of the membership—was incorporated under American law as Ballington had demanded.

But William Booth felt that his children had no business to resign. 'Confidence in God and in me' was still his principle. Thus when in 1912 he died, the sealed envelope was opened and Bramwell Booth his son—Mr Bramwell—reigned in his stead.

General Bramwell Booth guided the Army through the First World War. With his wife, the influential Florence Booth, he travelled the world, preached, wrote and prayed. Under his leadership the Army spread in Eastern Europe, Africa and the Far East. But the doom of the sealed envelope awaited him. It was widely believed that the Generalship might become hereditary in the house of Booth.

A mysterious 'W. L. Atwood' wrote from Wichita Falls, Texas, condemning the rule of 'dictators, czars, kaisers, emperors, pseudo-generals and numerous other self-appointed and hereditary leaders. . . . The General seems, like the Bourbons, to have learned nothing and forgotten nothing. The faithful warnings given him by loyal officers at the expense of exile and neglect worse than death have passed unheeded.'

Read between the lines, the London *War Cry* of the 1920s gives clear indication of a coming crisis. Students of the one-party state will recognize the symptoms: adulation of the leader to the point of embarrassment, reports of progress on all fronts, and a total absence of any criticism of the official line.

Bramwell's seventieth birthday was celebrated with a special number whose front cover depicted the aged William's charge to his son: 'to do more for the homeless, the world around, and to unfurl the Army flag in China'. The two were depicted, clasping hands, beneath a small picture of Catherine Booth.

But meanwhile, from the United States, Bramwell's sister, Commander Evangeline Booth, urged her brother to exercise his powers and make the Generalship elective. Readers of the *War Cry* were not informed of this. Only on 28 April 1928 did that paper report the General had had 'a slight attack of influenza'. The medical and constitutional crisis had gone much further, when, on 24 November 1928, the paper announced: 'The High Council to meet in London.' 'Discussion . . . as to supposed claimants to the Generalship are premature . . . the matter . . . can be decided only when a vacancy arises.' The statement did not add that, in order to bring about a vacancy, it would be necessary to remove the sitting incumbent.

The High Council of 1929 was a classic tragedy that still awaits the dramatist. The Seven against Bramwell—the requisitioning Commissioners—had no precedent to guide them. The rank and file knew little and were told less. General Bramwell Booth, from his sickbed at Southwold on the east coast of England, could only plead for time. Resign he would not, and by 55 votes to 8 he was deposed. Commissioner William Haines, the Council's Vice-President, collapsed and died. A High Court injunction in Bramwell's favour led only to another vote—and this time only five—four of whom were Booths—supported him. Four months later he was dead, and his funeral service packed London's Albert Hall to capacity.

The outcome of the crisis of 1929 was The Salvation Army Act of 1931 which (writes General Frederick Coutts) 'secured two fundamental changes in the Army's constitution. First of all it provided that it should be the duty of the High Council to elect a new General whenever the office became vacant, and in the second place, directed that a Salvation Army Trustee Company should be formed . . . to hold . . . all property . . . hitherto vested . . . in the General'.

And under this system the Army has operated ever since. The first tendency of the new system was to restrict the representative principle, for whereas the first High Council included Officers Commanding from all parts of the world, and embraced the relatively humble rank—in Army terms—of Brigadier—the later model admitted only Commissioners, Lieutenant-Commissioners, and Territorial Commanders who had held the rank of Colonel for at least two years. Not surprisingly therefore, successive High Councils have contained more men than women, more white people than black, more over-sixties than under-sixties, and no 'laity' at all. The Army is in fact ruled by a self-perpetuating oligarchy. However, since 1929 there has been a steady, if very slow, trend towards democracy. The complicated system of officers' ranks has been simplified. 'Senior Majors' have followed 'Ensigns' into oblivion. Advisory and consultative groups have sprung up—and in some cases withered away, for their effectiveness depends largely on the willingness of a Territorial Leader to be advised.

The provisions of The Salvation Army Act 1931 have remained in force, with amendments in 1965 and 1968. A major point of interest has been the retirement age of the General—held by Parliament to be an internal question. In 1975 General Wiseman, with the necessary consent of a two-thirds majority of the Commissioners, made a regulation whereby the General should in future cease to hold the position on reaching the age of 68—or after five years in office. Such an arrangement might in future make possible the election of a younger General—and turn the position into a kind of 'rotating presidency'. Whether it will do so remains to be seen.

Office bearers in The Salvation Army fall into two groups: 'officers' and 'local officers'. The latter are, in the language of other Christian bodies, 'laity' who hold a commission empowering them to undertake tasks that vary from holding large sums of local funds to teaching in the Sunday school. As always, local officers are appointed, not elected; they are presented with a commission signed by the Divisional Commander, on the recommendation of the local Commanding Officer. The local officers of The Salvation Army are its centurions—faithful and committed Christians who may range from the grizzled veteran who, for forty years and more, has taught generations of boys to play brass instruments—to the teenage girl who tackles the Sunday school while in the middle of her exams. If the Army hall is open seven nights a week, with activity for all ages and conditions of men—then that corps will turn out to be blessed with committed local officers. If the doors are shut from Sunday to Sunday—then probably the poor Captain will be tearing his (or her) hair because no one 'will take the positions'.

For the Army at local level is a voluntary movement, and the paradox of its constitution means that while the local congregation does not elect its leader, it does not have to take any notice of its leader either. You can always drag your feet, even if you don't vote with your feet. The man—or woman—at the point of intersection between Headquarters and the local fellowship is the 'corps officer'.

The full-time officers of The Salvation Army are successors to the evangelists of the East London Christian Mission. It was Evangelist Elijah Cadman who first called himself 'Captain'. Salvation Army officers are men and women who feel a call to give up their full-time occupation for the preaching of the gospel. After interview, selection process, 18 months' training in one of the Army's colleges —usually there is one per territory—they are commissioned: after making their vow 'for Christ's sake, to feed the poor, to clothe the naked, love the unlovable and befriend the friendless'. They are then appointed to preach the gospel—perhaps in a crowded city centre, perhaps in the remotest bush. Pay is low. In Britain it hovers around the Family Income Supplement level. Officership has always been open to both men and women, and some who come forward for training will be married couples who have sold up home and business. Others come single—and the Army's policy has always been that an officer may only marry another officer. Since there are in most countries more women candidates than men, some of the girls at least must either resign in order to marry, or accept the prospect of single life. The men are able to have it both ways.

For passing time has brought problems to Salvation Army officership as to other professions. As the Army's work developed, there were added to the simple mission station, homes, schools, and hospitals. Thus there developed the officer-nurse, the officer-teacher, the officer-doctor, the officer-accountant. But what precisely is the difference between—say an officer-nurse and an ordinary (Christian) nurse? Is it simply that the former does the same job for less pay? The temptations of status, rank and place-seeking are not unknown. The unscriptural distinction between 'staff' and 'field' officers has been got rid of, and the rank system simplified, but there still remains a ladder leading from Lieutenant to Captain, to Major . . . and so up—if 'up' is the word—to General. Some feel it would be better to go over to the Presbyterian tradition and have complete equality of ministers—only there, it would seem, some are more equal than others—and those with BDs are more equal than those without.

Which brings us to another problem: theological education. George Scott Railton was in full agreement with George Fox that being bred up at Oxford and Cambridge did not make anyone fit to be a minister of Christ. 'The air of the condescending curate', he wrote to his son—who became a curate—'always seems to me much more offensive than the vilest abuse of the low-class publican.' Thus it was always Army policy to accept for training the boy and girl with little formal education. 'Whilst we do not despise education', declared the future General Edward Higgins in 1929, 'we know from experience that the education of the heart is of far greater consequence than that of the mind in salvation work.'

But time would also play havoc with that truth—or half-truth. Medical personnel would require qualifications, teachers would need certificates, social workers seek diplomas. Even the field officer—the prototype Salvation Army officer in days when the world was young—would need to keep up with the rising standards of his people. Nobody ever intended, surely, that Salvation Army officer-ship should be for those who 'failed their standard six'

and could not get into the pupil teachers' centre! So
at last the Army comes round to minimum educational
standards—and, let us suppose, 'standard six pass' is the
minimum level required. But the world moves on, and by
now only 'Cambridge holders' (High School Graduates)
are eligible for teacher training. Poor old 'Standard Six
Pass' can either stay jobless or enter the ministry.

Again the unique structure of Salvation Army officership poses problems for the relationships between the
sexes. Equality between men and women—since Catherine
Booth's day this has been the Army's proudest boast. But
while it may be true theologically—for women can perform any religious rite that men perform—it is very
doubtful if it is true administratively. All the heartache
about keeping women in 'assistant', 'deputy' jobs, so
familiar in the world as a whole, can be found in The
Salvation Army. Buried in the files of the *Staff Review*
for 1930 is an anguished correspondence on the topic
'Are equal standards maintained?' The conclusion—
hardly to be avoided—is that they are not. The same
concern surfaced in *The Officer* during 1975—International women's year—forty-five years on.

For a peculiarity of The Salvation Army is that it rarely
gives a personal appointment to the *married* woman
officer at all. On 'the field'—and at times elsewhere—she
shares in and assists her husband's work. But if he comes
'off the field' she is left jobless. Meanwhile, the single
women soldier on. It looks like the classic pattern of
'divide and rule'—but to do anything about it would mean
a move from direction of labour to a free market—at
least for the married women officers. And that would
stand the Army's constitution on its head.

Yet in spite of the 'identity crisis' which affects officership like other branches of the Christian ministry, to
attend a Candidates Conference remains a profoundly

moving experience. To interview, one after another—an ex-RAF policeman, a twenty-two-year-old girl with dazzling good looks and a degree in sociology, a business man and his wife who are selling all that they have . . . what have these incongruous people in common save their love for an invisible God and their conviction that He has called them to serve their fellow-men? True discipleship differs little across the centuries, whether the disciple wears a linen robe, a homespun gown, or a navy blue uniform. At a Salvation Army Candidates' Conference, St Francis of Assisi would feel at home.

Which brings us to the ecumenical question. For the Salvationist the Church is first of all the people of God—the whole company of those who say 'yes' to Jesus Christ. It follows, therefore, that it exists in a multiplicity of denominations. Thus the Army has belonged to the World Council of Churches since that body was founded. But—peculiar constitution again—it is the world-wide movement that belongs, via the General and International Headquarters—and not the local territories. Hence a territory where conservative, anti-WCC views prevail cannot do much about it—unless the entire Army can be persuaded to leave. At local level The Salvation Army takes part in national Councils of Churches in most—though not all—parts of the world. But it has never taken part in any reunion negotiations such as brought about the Church of South India. Unity and not uniformity has been the ideal. 'If we are to receive one another', declared General Frederick Coutts, 'we must forget our imagined superiorities—our historical superiorities, which can be a besetting temptation for the older communions; or fancied spiritual superiorities, a besetting temptation of the younger bodies, including my own.' On another occasion he declared: 'There remains a large question-mark against administrative union. Rite and sacrament still sadly

divide . . . but salvation—this personal experience of
Christ as Saviour—this should surely unite us all.'

Hesitations over the Army's membership of the World
Council of Churches can be political as well as religious.
Few Salvationists would go as far as Senior Major Allister
Smith, who holds that 'in the WCC are conservatives
and liberals, Calvinists and Arminians, Communists,
Socialists, Liberals and Catholics hovering on the side-
lines and ready to take over and produce the false prophet
who will collaborate with the political antichrist soon
to emerge, possibly in the guise of Communism'. But in
General Albert Orsborn's time, in the 1950s, the Army
withdrew from the Central Committee for a time. The
same step was taken by General Wickberg during the
controversy over World Council of Churches grants to
insurgent organizations in Southern Africa. The Army—
which made no payment to the Fund to Combat Racism—
withdrew for a time from the WCC's Central Committee.
The reason for this action must be sought in the balance
of power within the Army itself. Withdrawal from the
Central Committee pleases the 'antis' while retention of
World Council of Churches membership placates the
'pros'. The price paid is the loss of any influence the
Army might have on WCC policy.

Co-operation then, and not union, has been the
Army's policy towards other churches, and it has resisted
attempts at mergers promoted by the State. In Korea,
Japan, and Zaire the Army has been more reluctant than
most denominations to join a State-sponsored United
Church. Indeed few Salvationists have really thought
hard about what might be involved. Mutual recognition
would be essential—that is obvious—and any benighted
churchman who regarded the Army as being outside the
fold would prove thereby nothing but his own ignorance.
But mutual recognition—as what? Salvationists can

recognize Roman Catholic priests, for example, as pastors, evangelists, fellow-disciples, Christian friends. They could hardly recognize them as priests in the sense intended by St Ignatius Loyola and the Council of Trent. Moreover, any attempt at church union raises for the Army all the problems faced when a small group with a distinctive culture is asked to combine with a larger one. Back in the seventeenth century the Reverend Robert Blair thought that the Union between England and Scotland would be the union of the poor bird with the hawk that devours it: a feeling not always appreciated by ecumenical Christians who may share a common educational and social background but a different denominational one.

Co-operation, friendship, charity . . . are surely something to be going on with. A next step for the Army could be to pay rather more than the minimum subscription to inter-Christian efforts and to contribute some of its manpower. There is still an inter-Church pecking order, which varies from country to country according to the size and wealth of the various Churches involved, but we have come a long way from the days when George Scott Railton could break his heart because 'if pressed I should have to admit that you' (his son David) 'spent part of the year studying at Oxford'.

Perhaps, in the end, it is a difference of social outlook and custom, rather than theology, that keeps Christians apart. The Territorial Commander in Scotland was once asked why there could not be, for an experimental period, a minister from another Church commissioned to work in The Salvation Army.

'A good idea', he said. 'No reason why not.' Then he added: 'We wouldn't want a reeking lum.'*

---

* A smoking chimney. The minister would have to be a non-smoker.

The Rules they Live by

None of the recruits at Ilford is a 'reeking lum'. Any Salvationist enrolled after 1976 must be a non-smoker, and 'no smoking' is one of the prohibitions which, together with teetotalism, make some unfriendly critics feel that Salvationist ethics consist mainly of 'don'ts'.

Throughout Christian history the Church has faced a dilemma: do you try to pack the people in and risk lowering standards? Or do you keep standards high and numbers low? Is the Church to be a Noah's ark containing beasts both clean and unclean, or an Army of the committed, prepared to travel light for the sake of the cause? One classic compromise was the 'two-class' Church: less was to be expected of lay people who could not possibly— so the theory ran—live up to the high standards of the religious professionals—priests, monks and nuns.

At the Reformation the idea of a two-class Church was rejected. Double standards were humbug, and all the faithful were called to be 'visible saints', born again through the Spirit and separated—if it came to that heartbreaking decision—from the half-hearted muster at the parish church. Hence the long and heroic effort of Puritanism. At the very time when Richard Burbage was playing in Shakespeare's *Hamlet* at the Globe Theatre, the pioneer congregationalists Barrow and Greenwood were awaiting execution in the Clink prison a few hundred yards away. 'Reformation without tarrying for anie' was to prove an explosive slogan.

But the problem with all religious revivals is how to

keep them going. The second generation of 'visible saints' may be less committed than the first, while the third may be almost indistinguishable from the establishment—in which unlikely quarter signs of grace may indeed appear. In seventeenth-century England even Oliver Cromwell failed to come up to scratch: 'His court was full of sin and vanity, and the more abominable, because they had not yet quite cast away the name of God, but profaned it. True religion was now almost lost, even among the religious party.'

So declared Lucy Hutchinson, with some bias, for her husband had died in prison for the Good Old Cause which others deserted. And in the next century, when the saints rode out to spiritual and no longer to carnal warfare, the Methodist revival attempted to realize yet again the ideal of New Testament Christianity. A hundred years further on, and George Scott Railton, Secretary of the Christian Mission, called for yet another attempt to show to the world the determination of the visible saints. One of his pamphlets was entitled *John Wesley, the Saved Clergyman*; and lest any should fail to realize that ordination by itself was useless, an engraving featured a sick-looking Wesley on a sloping deck with the caption 'The unsaved clergyman in the storm'.

As for the once-fiery Society of Friends, Railton lamented: 'Can it be that these quiet reserved gentlemen, whose meetings are now noted for nothing so much as for their silence, are followers of the men who stood up in churches . . . in graveyards, in market-places, and spoke, hour after hour, denouncing every form of sin in a way that made even great men quake with fear?'

The ethic of the Puritan, so often seen as mere negation, was never intended to be so. The morality of rigorist Christianity is that of an explorer on an enterprise very difficult, or of a soldier on active service. Its roots are plain in the New Testament itself. 'A soldier on active service will not let himself be involved with civilian affairs', says the letter to Timothy. 'He must be wholly at his commanding officer's disposal' (2 Timothy 2.4 NEB).

Such is the ideal at which Salvationist morality aims. 'The salvation soldier' declares Section 1 of the *Orders and Regulations* (1972 edition), 'must have been changed by the Holy Spirit from the old, worldly, selfish, sinful nature to a new nature. . . . It is impossible . . . to perform the duties hereafter set forth . . . unless a change of heart has been experienced. . . .'

The ethics of the Salvationists are therefore simply another attempt to reassert traditional Christian ethics, based on the New Testament. They are, of course, conditioned by the climate of opinion in which believers must live. At their best they succeed in realizing the ideal of the soldier on active service—equipped not to kill but to save. Of Salvationist moral concern at its worst we may recall what Professor Owen Chadwick said, not unkindly, of their predecessors in the seventeenth century: 'The moral discipline exercised by the congregation required much experience before it ceased to waste away in criticizing the whalebones in the petticoats of a pastor's wife.'

Salvationist ethics are therefore Christian ethics, teaching honesty, love, loyalty, moderation—and thrift.

Not for the first or the last time, therefore, does the Church of the disinherited come to inherit, if not the earth, at any rate a prosperous place in society. Gunpei Yamamuro, the great Japanese Salvationist whose *Common People's Gospel* ran to over 500 editions, was impressed, as a young man, by the Victorian classic *Self Help* by Samuel Smiles. It 'showed that the power of Christianity lay in its applicability to the practical needs of everyday life'.

Is it inevitable, then, that 'working-class' religious movements grow 'middle class' in the third generation? In Britain at least, the successor to the old Victorian Salvation Army must be sought among the black Churches of West Indian and African origin: the New Testament Church of God in Christ, the Cherubim and Seraphim, the Miracle Praying Band.

Turning to specific moral questions, we find that Quaker influence on the Army never extended to the adoption of Quaker principles about swearing oaths and waging war. There were indeed some who thought that the Army ought to embrace pacifism on principle. Arthur Booth-Clibborn, a tragic figure, wrote an impassioned tract called *Blood against Blood*. He was appalled—holy simplicity—by the carnage of the Boer War, and far from impressed by the promise included in the passes issued to members of the Army's Naval and Military League. 'By the grace of God I promise (1) Total abstinence. (2) Purity. (3) To discourage gambling. (4) To read daily from God's word. (5) To do my level best to bring my comrades to Christ.'

Booth-Clibborn commented: 'There is no promise to obey the command: thou shalt not kill.'

But Booth-Clibborn, though married to William Booth's eldest daughter, was an 'outsider', as was Herbert Booth by the time he embraced pacifism after the First World War. In *The Saint and the Sword* he wrote: 'If we Christians fail to make war against war with at least an equal valour as that manifested by those who risk their lives in defence of their country we . . . can hope for nothing but contempt for our message.'

Yet pacifism has remained a minority view within the Army, as indeed within the Church as a whole. Pacifists and conscientious objectors have certainly not been missing from the ranks. When conscription of ministers of religion was proposed in Britain, in 1918, S. C. Gauntlett —later to lead the shattered German Salvation Army after another world war—was prepared to go to jail over the issue, and commented with some irony. 'It would no doubt be reassuring to know that I could resume my Army service at the conclusion of the war or imprisonment.'

Sadly, the Army has been no more successful than other religious believers in drawing the line between just and unjust war, between maximum and minimum force, between police action and genocide: and this in spite of all the brave efforts for the serving soldier, the prisoner, the wounded and the refugee—efforts that have won it honourable public esteem. Booth-Clibborn was appalled at the thought of Boers and Britons bayoneting each other 'in sight of the heathen'. The Battle of the Somme was still to come, and so was Hiroshima.

First on the list of promises made by the Naval and Military Leaguers was 'total abstinence'. Here is the first of the great prohibitions that have often made the Army's ethics look like pure negation; the Salvationist being seen as one who neither smokes, drinks, nor gambles, and can dance no dance more complicated than The Grand Old Duke of York. Such emphases derive of course, from the evangelical and Methodist traditions: the promise of total abstinence being, until recently, the only one written into the *Articles of War*.

In 1922 the future General Evangeline Booth addressed the National Women's Christian Temperance Union in Philadelphia, USA, and declared: 'I stand here as leader of a Movement that, in its attitude towards the drink evil, has never known a hesitating moment. At the inception of The Salvation Army . . . prohibition was in its infancy, and there was then no condemnation of moderate drinkers. A religious movement, with total abstinence as a condition of membership, was both novel and unpopular.

But . . . our Founder, my father, saw this was the curse that bound the poor man as with an iron chain to his poverty. Proscription was the only course, and that course, without a single exception has been followed . . . we stand today as the greatest temperance movement on the face of the earth.'

As Evangeline Booth conceded, it had not been so at the beginning. When the mission began, both tea and coffee were expensive and troublesome to prepare. Beer was the common drink of the London poor—and beer, and worse still, spirits, were too often their downfall. 'On Saturday night, after the workmen's weekly pay had been taken—it was a revolting sight for a sensitive man to witness the ghastly scenes at the tavern doors. Drunken men by the hundred lay about higgledy-piggledy in the mud, hollow-eyed and purple-cheeked, their ragged clothing plastered with muck.' Catherine Booth, who knew what she was talking about, spoke of East Londoners whose 'mental faculties are so benumbed by the imbruting drink, that a vacant stare is often the only response to the first attempt at arousing and reclaiming them'.

Both she and her husband William were shocked, therefore, when members of the Christian Mission, on an outing to the East Londoners' playground—Epping Forest—'ate their lunch on tables outside a public house and had beer with their meal. Mrs Booth . . . took loose tea and obtained boiling water, at a charge of 2d per head'.

But the mission as a whole would not be persuaded to sign the pledge without some resistance. At the 1876 conference a proposal to make total abstinence a condition of membership had to be watered down. William Booth himself was quite clear that he wanted a religious movement, not a temperance society. 'We will have no mere teetotalism', he declared, 'we will teach our people never to drink or touch the stuff, *for Christ's sake.*'

Total abstinence became a condition of membership when the *Articles of War* were introduced in 1882. Once again it turns out to be in the five years following 1878 that a 'typically Army' emphasis appears. Even the *Orders and Regulations* (1878) had spoken only of 'the almost universal adoption of the principle by our people generally'. The move to total abstinence was, of course, part of the great temperance movement of the late nineteenth century, whose finest hour was in 1919, with the 18th amendment to the constitution of the United States. Of prohibition it has been said: 'In the complex of values which has characterized the American middle classes self-mastery, industry, thrift and moral conduct have been . . . prized. . . . Self-denial has been viewed as a necessary step to the achievement of social and economic success . . . the ascetic strain in American Protestantism has tended to make for a perfectionist's bent in American religion . . . and a disposition to perfect the wayward, the weak and the alien' (Article: 'Prohibition', *Encyclopaedia Britannica*, 1969 ed.).

The Army in the United States did all it could to support prohibition, short of actively backing prohibitionist candidates—the *War Cry* looking forward 'to the time when every drop of rum, whisky, and lager shall have been emptied into the right place—the gutter'. With the passing of the 18th amendment, the Army was even able to drop its annual Boozers Day—for the disappearance of drink meant, it was claimed, the disappearance of drunks.

But the great experiment would fail. Already in 1922 Evangeline Booth's lecture to the Women's Christian Temperance Union had an ominous title: *Shall America go back?* Expecting the answer: no, her purple prose received the answer: yes. In 1933 prohibition was repealed —at least one gangster having been shot dead outside

Army Headquarters in Chicago. The supreme effort of the visible saints had failed, and the sons of Belial were left in possession of the field.

But not in undisputed possession—and perhaps the saints, like their predecessors in the seventeenth century, had been fighting the wrong battle with the wrong weapons. Prohibition will work only if public opinion will stand for it—and Salvationists can at least claim to be consistent. The claims of those who would like to legalize marijuana—why ban pot if you don't ban booze?—cut no ice with people who abstain from both.

But just what constitutes booze? Precise definition is difficult. Does it include palm wine—freshly tapped, fermenting or 'dead'? Why is small beer not considered alcoholic at the Maison du Jeune Homme in Paris? More dangerous than such questions of definition are the doubts that arise in some minds at least as to the rightness of the Army's stand. The drink trade's propaganda is directed towards the young: it portrays alcohol as helpful, friendly, the right thing to indulge in. Is the pledge to total abstinence a Victorian relic? Is it something one accepts for the good of the cause? Secret drinkers are, no doubt, few and far between, but great grief can be caused to the sensitive conscience by the total abstinence clause in the *Articles of War*. 'But sir,' says a young recruit, 'XYZ drinks!!' There seems to be no answer to that.

'Never to drink or touch the stuff . . . for Christ's sake . . .' William Booth's ideal makes clear that the Army's no drinking rule must go hand in hand with a loving ministry to the alcoholic. And this the Army, world wide, certainly attempts to provide. Angus, born in Lewis, has lost the Gaelic but not the lilting English of the Western Isles: he went to sea and drink was his downfall . . . the Army has looked after him on Roto Roa Island off the coast of New Zealand, and in Whitechapel,

London. Angus, with the Army's help, just about keeps his head above water—or above the whisky.

But the Army's anti-alcoholism programme is usually carried out by small groups of specialists: the rank and file Salvationist too often knows little or nothing about it. The coming generation will need to be convinced of the rightness and usefulness of total abstinence as a part of Christian living: if not, the Army will have the same problems with alcohol that the Pope has with the contraceptive pill.

On smoking, public opinion has moved, in the West at least, in the opposite direction. It is now much less fashionable to smoke, and in Britain the cigarette packet, not the whisky bottle, carries a government health warning. Salvationist smokers are few and far between, but until 1975 the rule was that only officers and local officers were required to abstain. In that year the Commissioners' Conference recommended that non-smoking should be made compulsory for all future soldiers. How far this change carries the judgment of the rank and file is difficult to determine. Where the Army derives most of its recruits from its own young people, raised in a no-smoking environment, there may well be little to worry about. Where converts are won from 'outside', the struggle to give up smoking can be cruel—and the Commissioners' decision, now implemented, will not make it any easier.

Like all the Christian Churches, the Army has had to cope with the sexual revolution. It inherited the traditional evangelical and Christian morality about sex. The naval and military leaguer, vowed to 'purity' was presumably committed to abstain from fornication, masturbation, pornography and dirty jokes. 'The salvation soldier', say the *Orders and Regulations* for 1899, 'must not place his hands in a familiar manner on any person, or kiss anyone of the opposite sex, unless it is a relative or some person to whom he is engaged.'

This rule was a subject of teenage derision by the 1950s. No kissing before engagement went out—if it was ever in —more than a generation ago. And the old reticence about purity has given way to a culture—at least in the West and increasingly world wide—which inculcates sex-with-everything. Not for nothing does the Army's Major Stephen Ng, in collaboration with a Catholic priest, head the anti-pornography drive in Hong Kong. He looks with mixed feelings across to the Chinese People's Republic, where they ban dirty books—but you can't sell Bibles either.

But Christian hangups over sex are often exaggerated, and the Puritans often turn out to be less kinky than some of their critics. Any sexual relationship for the Christian is, after all, an eternal triangle between man, woman and God, and those who know nothing of the third party, may well misunderstand the relationship between the other two.

Because of traditional reticence or prudery it is difficult to document changing attitudes towards sex. In 1927 the redoubtable A. G. Cunningham published a pamphlet entitled *Personal Purity*. Young men with purity problems were advised to sleep with a cotton reel fastened round the waist. In the early 1930s Hollywood began to make its presence felt. In 1933 A. J. Gilliard noted that the new cinema brought temptations unknown to the old music hall, and that the rule about strict separation from worldly amusement was beginning to slip: 'to exploit the most unruly of human instincts . . . writers who supply screen notes can use the initials "SA" without fearing that their readers will be puzzled over the introduction of references to South Africa or The Salvation Army'. (The editor explained, to the uninitiated, that 'SA' stood for sex appeal.)

Meanwhile, in the West, the Christian ideal of married love, so admirably demonstrated by William and Catherine Booth, came under increasing attack. In other parts of the world it had never been accepted in the first place. Ancient conundrums—and newer ones—are sent in to the West African *War Cry*.

'Is there any harm in knowing the sex of our girls before marrying them?'

'Does The Salvation Army support birth control by using contraceptives?'

'Conditions in Africa are quite different from those in European countries. Will it be wrong for a polygamous Salvationist who really feels the call of God to take up any office in a West African corps?'

Whether The Salvation Army supported birth control by using contraceptives was far from clear for some years. The practice must have been widely accepted by the rank and file long before any official statement was made. This was in fact the teaching of the Christian Medical Association of India, given the General's blessing in 1961. . . . Here the aims of Christian marriage are defined as:

(*a*) the procreation of children.

(*b*) mutual companionship and help

(*c*) the right use of the natural instincts of men and women.

The Indian medical men—who should know all about over-population—accept that contraception has a legitimate place in marriage; they allow sterilization on reasonable grounds, but record 'strong disapproval of abortion as a means of controlling the number of children'.

And the Army has continued to disapprove of easy abortion. In 1967 General Coutts called for a Royal Commission to halt the progress of the Abortion Bill through the British parliament. It is hardly surprising that a body of people vowed to befriend the friendless and feed the hungry should find abortion on demand offensive and wrong. Now, in many countries which are permissive towards abortion, Salvationists are among the conscientious opposition. 'Widespread abortion', wrote lawyer and Salvation Army officer, Shaw Clifton, in 1974, 'must eventually have a dehumanizing effect on any society that encourages it.' But is the foetus a baby? Has it got a soul? On this critical question Clifton writes: 'We have to give the foetus an extremely high value, as high as that given to human life in general, so that the burden of proving the morality of ending the life of a foetus in any given case rests squarely on the one claiming the exception to the general rule.'

What does the Army do about the remarriage of divorced persons? It can no longer be claimed that marital break-down is so rare among Salvationists as to constitute no problem. Lifelong love between man and woman—'they lived happily ever after'—is still the natural expectation of young Salvationists, but even among them, grace does not always prevail: and it is possible, at least, for divorced persons to be remarried in the Army hall and for remarried persons to be commissioned as officers. Here the rigorists are found, not among Salvationists, but in the ranks of the Roman Catholics and the Anglicans.

On the other hand, the Army has always taken an absolute stand on gambling. The Orders and Regulations clearly regard gambling as wrong in principle and not simply when indulged in to excess. Gambling, writes General F. Coutts, is 'a sin against, God, myself, society and my neighbour', since it is an attempt to profit at his expense. Even if gambling profits my pocket, someone else must lose, 'for as we teach our people that there are no "large" sins or "small" sins, but that all sin is sin in the sight of God, so whether I give the office boy sixpence for a ticket for his bicycle raffle, or lay £5 on the cash

desk of a totalizator at Epsom race course, I contravene
the moral law that is utterly opposed to all forms of
gambling'.

Scandinavia turns out to be a large pocket of resistance
to this point of view. Here the Army regularly raises
money by means of raffles, and in 1973, for example, the
Army's nationwide lottery in Norway put up ten Opel
Kadetts as prizes. Tickets 5 kroner—all in aid of the new
Jeløy Folk High School.

Those who sit in the seat of the scornful may well mock
the visible saints over such inconsistencies as this. Like
everyone else, the Army has at times been guilty of making
the word of God of none effect through its traditions.
Young consciences may be pained for little reason over
the sinfulness of buying ice-cream on Sunday, or wearing
lipstick with a bonnet, or drinking pepsi-cola in a pub.

'It was on furlough that we met her', writes a corre-
spondent in an Army paper, 'full uniform, smart and a
good mother—for that was obvious by the way her
children were cared for. But why did she have to wear
light blue eye shadow? Her looks did not need any
enhancing. Was it really necessary?'

No doubt it wasn't—but was it necessary to write to the
paper about it?

But while ice-cream on Sundays, lipstick with bonnets
and pepsi-cola in pubs may be the small change of moral
concern, they are none the less real and painful dilemmas
for those who face them. The old idea of separation from
the world meant that the believer centred his life totally
on the Christian community, and created an entire culture
there. Hence the phenomenal growth of Salvation Army
music-making. Hence too the relative neglect of drama—
for the Army inherited the old evangelical idea of the
'absolute unlawfulness of stage plays'. It is true that
Herbert Booth, at the beginning of the century, pioneered

the religious film, but plays were called 'demonstrations' until recently.

There were also strong suspicions of sport in earlier days—this may well have had something to do with class feeling—for organized games were the preserve of the idle rich. In this, before 1914, the Army differed little from other Christian groups of the day. A critic wrote: 'Rigid attempts are made by . . . International Head-quarters . . . and other religious houses in the city (of London) to impose a code of morals that violates all sense of proportion . . . no encouragement is given to healthy outdoor games or rifle or gymnastic exercises.' Twenty years later Colonel Percy Turner, pioneer medical missionary in India, had to contend for the lawfulness of football as a Christian pastime: 'One thing that has embittered and estranged from the Army many intelligent and active young people', he wrote, 'has been the attitude of some of the older generation towards even healthy and beneficial forms of exercise.'

All that has long changed—once the Army began to open schools it had to change. In Nigeria, for example, the Army produced a national 400 metres champion who might have been Olympic material if the civil war had not broken out. But if the idea of social separation is no longer possible or even desirable, then the duty of moral discrimination becomes even more pressing. It may not be a sin nowadays to go to the pictures—television finally put paid to all that—but is it a sin to go and see *Soldier Blue*? or *A Clockwork Orange*? or *Confessions of a Window Cleaner*? My under-age friends all go to 'X' films. So what am I to do?

The yoke of Christ may be easy, but it still has to be worn. Christians may be called on, not only to renounce evil, but to give up the good for the sake of the best. It is a dilemma about which our recruits will have thought long and hard before they signed their *Articles of War*.

And the yoke of Christ will prove far from easy if the wearer is not sustained by an inward and personal faith. Our recruits at Ilford differ widely in age and outlook: Salvationists around the world are even more various— but they all agree about the reality of spiritual experience. God exists—and man can communicate with Him.

CHAPTER FOUR

Their Inward Faith

Communion with God is the heart of the Salvationist's faith. Even a sympathetic observer—George Bernard Shaw—managed to miss this point completely. His 'Major Barbara'—a young lady from high society who joins The Salvation Army in its pioneering days—resigns her commission because she finds that the movement must take tainted capitalist money in order to help the hungry. At last, however, Barbara returns to the colours. 'I have got rid of the bribe of bread', she cried. 'I have got rid of the bribe of heaven. Let God's work be done for its own sake ... when I die, let Him be in my debt, not I in His.'

Shaw's play ends on a note which is good Shavianism but bad Salvationism. What devout Christian ever thought that God could be in debt to man? Compare and contrast the Major Barbara of the play with a similar heroine from real life: the ex-débutante Mildred Duff who went to work in London slums and ended up as a Salvation Army Commissioner:

'She rose with us at 4 a.m. and helped to prepare and serve the cocoa. Before the first lot of pale shabby children went back into the cold, she was ill with distress for them. It came to her that it was an everyday thing for British boys and girls to be sent hungry to school. . . .

'The Major sank on her knees beside the table. Her prayer was indeed a speaking to God because she knew Him as a friend; she could bring the sense of His presence to all who knelt with her. The divine light seemed to shine through the gloom of a hard winter in the slums. . . . A warm handshake, a God bless you, a radiant smile, and she was gone' (*Mildred Duff*, by Madge Unsworth, Salvationist Publishing and Supplies).

The inward motivation that one misses in Shaw's Barbara was obvious to Mildred Duff's companions. The latter's distress for the boys and girls with no breakfast arose from her personal commitment, not to the Life Force, but to a God of love.

A century later—and the scene has changed, while the situation remains. 'For us it is increasingly difficult', wrote the Dutch missionary, Major Eva den Hartog, from Bangladesh in November 1975, 'to face the fact that so many people have to die . . . we just do what we can to help the mothers and their starving children . . . I myself have come to the point that in cases where I can see no hope . . . I feel that the patient should simply be given loving care and as much comfort as possible, and the rest should be left to God. It is my vocation to be alert, and to understand what God wants me to do.'

Salvationist spirituality is active, rather than contemplative. It turns from the beatific vision to the nightmare of human need. And here, of course, it is by no means unique. For it is simply Christian piety, nourished through centuries of concern and going back to the Founder of the faith and His profoundest parables. 'Heart to God and hand to man'—this North American slogan is a good expression of the Army's ideal. How perfectly that ideal is realized in personal living is of course another question.

Any search for the religious roots of Salvationism must begin with the Methodism from which the Army sprang. This was the radical Methodism which had moved away from Wesley's Anglican origins. The Wesleyans retained the Anglican morning service but had preaching instead of evensong. The Primitives had a preaching service both night and morning. Their religion was stiffened by strong

doses of John and Charles Wesley's hymns. What effect
did the faith of those hymns have on the pioneer Salvationists—on able and original and generally untrained minds?

Consider the case of William Pearson.

Pearson, born in 1832 and a Christian Missioner in
1874—was the first publisher of the *War Cry*. When The
Salvation Army butterfly emerged from the Christian
Mission cocoon Pearson was enthusiastic. He composed
some of the Army's popular militant marching songs.
Having heard 'Ring the bell, watchman' played by the
bells of Bradford Town Hall, he wrote the following:

> Come, join our Army, to battle we go,
> Jesus will help us to conquer the foe;
> Fighting for right and opposing the wrong,
> The Salvation Army is marching along.

Pearson was, it seems, a good man to deal with a
difficult committee. 'He would get his leaders and elders
together and have a red hot prayer meeting . . . then,
when he had screwed them up to the highest pitch, and
made them in faith and love ready for anything, he would
tell them that he had a little business to go through. . . .'

Twenty-two of Pearson's songs feature in the Army's
current Song Book, and of these four in a row—numbers
553–556—plead for more zeal all round.

> Lord, give me more soul-saving love,
> Send a revival from above,
>   Thy mighty Spirit pour.
> The Army of salvation bless
> With righteousness and holiness,
>   Pressed down and running o'er.

Pearson got his metre—two lines of eight syllables and
followed by one of six—straight from *Wesley's Hymns*.

He would have appeared to have got his sentiments from the 'Believers Fighting' section of that famous book.

> Still will I strive, and labour still,
> With humble zeal to do Thy will,
> And trust in Thy defence;
> My soul into Thy hands I give,
> And, if he can obtain Thy leave,
> Let Satan pluck me thence.

(Charles Wesley)

More about Pearson the poet and Pearson the composer can be learned by comparing one of Wesley's greatest hymns with his imitation of it. John Wesley wrote:

> Give me the faith which can remove
> And sink the mountain to a plain;
> Give me the childlike praying love
> Which longs to build Thy house again;
> Thy love let it my heart o'erpower,
> And all my simple soul devour.

Pearson tries the same idiom. He loves the Lord as ardently as Wesley did, but his material is all over the place. . . .

> Give me the faith that Jesus had,
> The faith that can great mountains move,
> That makes the mournful spirit glad,
> The saving faith that works by love;
> The faith for which the saints have striven,
> The faith that pulls the fire from Heaven.

To pile up subordinate clauses for verse after verse may well prove difficult! Pearson is heading for a fall!:

> Give me the faith that lives to trust,
> That in the childlike spirit dwells,
> That buries self and slaughters lust,
> That keeps out all that Christ expels;

That gives no quarter to the foe,
That sternly says: You'll have to go.

The sad anti-climax of the last line shows that Pearson,
like Shakespeare in some of the sonnets, had trouble getting the last rhyme right. A more creditable Shakespearean
characteristic, and a clue to Pearson's inward religion, is
his use of the direct and concrete metaphor:

I want the faith that wears,
That can Jehovah see,
That glad life's heaviest burden bears,
That grips eternity.

The faith that will rejoice,
To saints by Jesus given,
That turns the key of Paradise
And saves from earth to Heaven.

That Pearson gripped eternity we do not doubt, and
he was not afraid to describe his awareness of God in the
bold erotic metaphors of the Song of Songs and St John
of the Cross.

Through the tempest, through the calm,
With the Master talking;
On my own Beloved's arm,
Oft with Jesus walking.

Through my thoughts and through my heart,
Through my flesh and spirit;
Save me, Lord, through every part,
Through Thy saving merit.

The Colonel's longing for salvation through every part
reminds us that any study of Salvationist spirituality must

consider its relationship, both negative and positive, with the Wesleyan doctrine of entire sanctification.

This the pioneer Salvationists were determined to maintain against all comers. They enshrined it in their Articles of Faith, with a rider added by Railton for those who failed to get the message. As the desire to holiness fell off, in their opinion, so love for the salvation of souls would diminish as well.

'Christian perfection', declared John Wesley is 'the loving God with all our heart, mind, soul and strength. This implies that no wrong temper, none contrary to love, remains in the soul.' But how could it come about? 'As to the manner, I believe that this perfection is always wrought in the soul by a simple act of faith—consequently in an instant. But I believe a gradual work, both preceding and following that instant . . . this instant generally is the instant of death, the moment before the soul leaves the body. But I believe it may be ten, twenty or forty years before.'

Wesley insisted that the moment of entire sanctification was in principle instantaneous—even though he granted that some of the saints might not notice it happening. He had no difficulty in quoting some of his brother's sublimest hymns in support.

> Now let me gain perfection's height,
> Now let me into nothing fall,
> Be less than nothing in Thy sight,
> And find that Christ is all in all.

His critics naturally accused the Wesley brothers of preaching sinlessness and encouraging vain self-confidence and spiritual pride. But the early Salvationists felt it their duty to reassert the pure Methodist doctrine. With their insistence on personal experience, they tended to stress the subjective side of it. 'Entire sanctification'—'The

Blessing'—as they called it, was a profound personal experience, similar in intensity to conversion but following conversion, which was consequent on an act of total self-surrender and renunciation. This belief has been potent among many of the Churches and religious groups that have sprung from the Wesleyan tradition, some of whom have associated the experience of sanctification with 'signs following'—claiming that the baptism of the Holy Spirit is validated by the power to speak in tongues. Once this step is taken, we arrive at Pentecostalism. But The Salvation Army has always refused to take this step.

This is not because nobody has ever spoken in tongues. Bramwell Booth could recall numerous occasions on which signs and wonders had occurred. Back in 1878 for example, 'we commenced an all night of prayer. . . . The power of the Holy Ghost fell on Robinson and prostrated him. He nearly fainted twice. The Brother of the Blandy's entered into full liberty' (i.e. he underwent the experience of entire sanctification) 'and then he shouted, wept, clapped his hands, danced amid a scene of the most heavenly and glorious enthusiasm . . . others were lying prostrate on the floor, some of them groaning aloud for perfect deliverance. . . .'

But there was never any chance that the Army would move into Pentecostalism or make the gift of tongues a required or even a desirable sign of a saint. 'Although some of our people have received what is spoken of as a gift of tongues, we have almost invariably found that one of the consequences has been a disposition to withdraw from hard work for the blessing of others and from fearless testimony to the Saviour.' Bramwell was General when he wrote that in 1925. The General had spoken, the case was finished.

But if the Army was cautious about 'signs following' it continued to uphold the doctrine of Entire Sanctification

—Methodist, Christian and Scriptural. And here it found a theologian in the shape of the American: Samuel Logan Brengle.*

As a student at Boston Theological Seminary, Brengle had belonged to the Octagon Club—a group which sought, like Wesley's Holy Club at Oxford, for Christian perfection. Brengle finds he knows the terminology, he has had a religious upbringing—but the experience eludes him. He seeks total surrender to the will of God. He prays:

'Lord, I want to be an eloquent preacher . . . but if by stammering and stuttering I can bring greater glory to Thee than by eloquence, then let me stammer and stutter.' This is the act of total self-denial which ought to be followed by the inrush of the Holy Spirit. But nothing happens. In a state of mental anticlimax Brengle realizes that the feeling of mental letdown is intended as a test for his soul. A promise comes into his mind. 'If we confess our sins, He is faithful and just to forgive us our sins, and to cleanse us from all unrighteousness.' He must accept santification as a man accepts salvation, by faith alone. 'Lord, I believe that', he declares and finds peace of soul, but no joy.

Two days later, as though in response to his faith, comes the joy. 'I walked over Boston Common before breakfast, weeping for joy and praising God. O how I loved. In that hour I knew Jesus, and I loved Him till it seemed my heart would break with love. I was filled with love for all His creatures. I heard the little sparrows chattering; I loved them. I saw a little worm wriggling over my path I stepped over it. I didn't want to hurt any living thing. I loved the dogs, I loved the horses, I loved the little urchins on the street, I loved the strangers who hurried past me. I loved the world.'

* Samuel Logan Brengle, DD, 1860–1936, Born in Fredericksburg, Indiana. Brengle was a Methodist who joined The Salvation Army in its pioneering period.

Was this the mere emotionalism of the moment? Forty years later Brengle wrote. 'I have never doubted the experience since . . . any more than I could doubt that I had seen my mother or looked at the sun or had my breakfast. It is a living experience. . . . In time God withdrew some of the tremendous emotional feelings. He taught me that I had to live by faith and not by my emotions, to have confidence in His unfailing love and devotion, no matter how I felt.'

Brengle's sanctification was to be tested soon, for he crossed the Atlantic to offer himself to William Booth and the Army, only to be told: 'Brengle you belong to the dangerous classes. You have been your own boss for so long that I do not think you will want to submit to Salvation Army discipline.'

But Brengle did submit, and produced in 1896, a book called *Helps to Holiness*. For a generation or more, this was to influence the spiritual life of the Army.

'Holiness', writes Brengle, 'is perfect love, a state in which there is no anger, malice, blasphemy, hypocrisy, envy, love of ease . . . a state in which there is no longer any doubt or fear . . . a state in which God is loved and trusted with a perfect heart.' The two great obstacles to holiness are (according to Brengle) imperfect consecration and imperfect faith. An example of the former is the poor backslider who admits that God called him to give up tobacco. God called him to renounce it, but he refused, 'and now he walks the streets a common drunkard, on the road to hell'. As for imperfect faith, even St Paul had to face it among his own people, for he told the Thessalonians that he prayed night and day to 'perfect that which is lacking in your faith'.

But only—if only—that total surrender of the will is made, then there will follow 'the inward revelation of the mind and heart of Jesus, through the baptism of the Holy

Ghost'. This may not occur immediately—for even Brengle had waited—but in God's good time.

Clearly Brengle's version of the holy life is pure Methodism, with the 'blessing' to be thought of as a definite experience, later than conversion and following on entire self-surrender. Equally clearly it does not move all the way to Pentecostalism, with the gift of prophecy or tongues as a sign of the Spirit's indwelling. Lastly, it was thought out well before the 'psychological revolution'. It knows nothing of anxiety states, phobias and neuroses. The young housewife, confined with two small children on the fifth floor of a block of flats—how shall she achieve that inward peace which is one of the marks of sanctification? Brengle does not tell us.

As years and generations go by, the thinkers and teachers of one generation begin to seem more and more irrelevant to the learners of the next. Thus it was with the Army, and its traditional idea of holy living. How frequently do forms of application filled in by 'Army' boys and girls require them to state the date of their conversion! Brought up not in the gutter but in the warmth of a home full of love human and divine, how often are they puzzled by the dotted line confronting them? But printed forms are not the only kinds of literature that outlast their relevance. Brengle's books began to gather dust on the shelves of Salvationist Publishing and Supplies, and his ideas began to grow dusty in the minds even of those who still knew them . . . until the charismatic movement of the 1970s brought the language of religious crisis back into fashion. The whirligig of time brings in its revenges—even in theology.

For even if the inward experience is by definition beyond words each generation of believers must struggle to find some language in which to convey it. Brengle's encounter with God on Boston Common was understood by him as

'The baptism of the Holy Spirit'. Among the Salvationists of the 1950s, to some of whom the idea of a 'second blessing' was as outdated as the dear old Brigadier's concertina, some new interpretation was called for. 'The question is sometimes asked,' wrote Frederick Coutts in *The Call to Holiness* 'whether the experience of holiness is gained instantly or gradually. The answer is that the life of holiness is both a crisis and a process'. He has borrowed the 'crisis and process' idea, he explained, from Bishop Handley Moule of Durham.

Comparing General Coutts' book with the writings of Brengle, one is struck by differences both of method and presupposition. *The Call to Holiness*—originally a series of Thursday night sermons at Camberwell—embodies the devout middle-of-the-road scholarship of British biblical theologians as C. H. Dodd and T. W. Manson. A critical approach to the Bible is everywhere assumed and nowhere proclaimed. Linguistic evidence is brought in to trace the development of the idea of the holy from primitive tabu to moral righteousness. Revelation is seen as progressive through the Old Testament and as culminating in Christ. Holiness is defined as 'Christlikeness' and expounded in the Pauline categories of love, joy, peace, longsuffering, goodness, faithfulness, meekness and temperance. Jesus is presented both as human example and indwelling Lord. The keywords are still religious, not psychological, and yet the writer is aware that mental pain can be as real as sin. A faith is offered that is both humane, liberal and deeply devout. 'Christian holiness is more than poise, though he who knows Christ within will know a heart's repose. It is more than the cultivation of courtesy . . . this experience is nothing less than the final dethronement of self and the infilling of the surrendered life to the spirit of Him who is the summation of all virtue.'

Coutts and Brengle share one characteristic typical of
the Army: the stress on 'experience'. For them as for
Salvationists generally, holiness is as much a personal
experience as an objective state of the soul. And this
common emphasis persists when we discover that there
are, within the Army, as many different approaches to the
life of the Spirit as there are types of people. We find, for
example, the quiet mysticism of the poet Catherine Baird:

> One startled moment came the heavens near,
> So near, so aweful that I ceased to hear,
> Inhale or taste, or feel or even see
> Aught time had promised for delight or dread . . .
> A lonely moment when the heavens came near . . .
> A perfect instant bright with God complete,
> To test my days and hours in furnace heat
> Till all that cannot live in fire be dead.
>
> *Reflections*, p. 9.

Are we back with Brengle on Boston Common? Here,
once more, is evident the experiential nature of Salvationist spirituality. In a footnote Catherine Baird has defined
her 'moment of truth' '. . . the hour when, in spite of
opposition and even of false witness, we are enabled by
God's grace to stand by what we believe to be true. In
such an hour of testing, God came'.

He did not come, we may note, in the sacrament of the
altar. The spirituality of the Salvationist is of necessity
non-sacramental. Human communion must replace holy
communion. As Albert Orsborn wrote:

> My life must be Christ's broken bread,
>   My love His outpoured wine,
> A cup o'erfilled, a table spread
>   Beneath His name and sign,
> That other souls, refreshed and fed,
>   May share His life through mine.

And that dedication can be expressed with infinite variety. Consider for example, the Indonesian Salvationist Jacobus Corputty, who for Christ's sake twice refused the regency of his native Rumakhai.

'God in His mercy turned my feet towards the army hall, I sat at the back and listened to the chorus:

> He takes me as I am
> My only plea, Christ died for me
> He takes me as I am.

The next Sunday I was born again. The words of Jesus challenged me 'Seek ye first the kingdom of God. . . .' When I was on the point of leaving for the training college in Bandung, Java, I was summoned to the office of the Regent of Surabaja, to be told that my father was dying and that the people of Rumakhai wanted me to return to take up the duties of Regent. I firmly declined, . . . the ship left Surabaja without me and an uncle was chosen . . . in my stead.'

The young Indonesian had previously considered 'The Salvation Army to be a kind of puppet show' and 'did not agree with handclapping, feeling that it brought dishonour to the living God'. He was won round by the friendly concern of local Salvationists, and *his* moment of truth came when they sang—of all things—a refrain by Ira D. Sankey, altered by oral tradition, exported from America via Britain to Indonesia and there translated. Would you give up an ancestral throne for one of Ira D. Sankey's gospel hymns? Perhaps not—but what if the sentimental refrain mediates the Lord of Glory in Person?

Meanwhile in Nigeria, the Salvationist's faith, like that of other Christians, must be worked out in accordance with even more ancient patterns of living and loving.

'I married when I was of age', writes Ajao in *The War Cry*, 'and it was a pity that this was not immediately

followed by the blessing of a baby. I prayed to God daily
about my standing problem. . . . I went to the doctor's
for a check up and they found that I was not sick. One day
I will ever remember. After my anxiety and daily crying
to the Lord, He answered my prayers. . . . He spoke to my
heart that my prayers were answered. I returned to my
quarters with a smiling face, believing that I had met my
Lord Jesus. . . . A few weeks later I reported to the doctor
who confirmed that I was expecting a baby. When it was
the time to deliver, I gave birth to a baby girl. . . . When
the child was eight days old she was named Oluwayemisi
which means "God remembered me".'

How strangely the traditional jargon of evangelical
Christianity ('my personal communion with the Lord
helped me') combines with primeval African and biblical
ways of thought! Not the sparrows on Boston Common,
but the first signs of pregnancy are the sacrament of
mercy. Hannah made a vow in these words: 'O Lord of
Hosts, if Thou wilt . . . but grant me offspring, then I will
give the child to the Lord for his whole life, and no razor
shall ever touch his head.' 'And she conceived' (according
to the first Book of Samuel, chapter 1) 'and in due time
bore a son whom she called Samuel, because she said "I
asked the Lord for him".'

And like Samuel, the little Oluwayemisi is named on
the eighth day, with the traditional Yoruba rite in which
her lips are touched with honey for sweetness, bitter kola
for strength, and salt to give her industry.

Brengle, Coutts, Baird, Orsborn, Corputty, Ajao—are
they united in a common faith or merely in a common
delusion? The twentieth century is sceptical about the
value of intuitive knowledge and calls for it to be cashed
at the counters of the secular world. Suppose that Ajao's
father was an animist, she herself may be a Christian of
animistic outlook. Her daughter, Oluwayemisi, may, if

intellectually inclined, become an agnostic, like at least one Nigerian student, while reading H. G. Wells in the reference library in some industrial English town. Salvationists stake so much on religious experience that their dilemma is all the more cruel when the validity of that experience is called in question. . . .

And yet, maybe the citadel is impregnable for those who find their way into it. In 1923 R. H. Thouless wrote: 'It is probable that the extent to which the psychological study of religion has power to dissolve religious faith has been exaggerated. When the psychologist describes what he believes to be the mental laws by which such an event as a conversion takes place, he in no way excludes the explanation that would be given by The Salvation Army, —that it takes place by the grace of God. To one who is sure that he has the vision of God, the scientific psychologist of religion can be no more than a blind man talking about colours' (*An Introduction to the Psychology of Religion*, p. 9).

Our six recruits at Ilford are in no doubt about the reality of the soul's communion with God. They have reaffirmed the classic Methodist doctrine of assurance: 'He that believeth hath the witness in himself.' But they also stand beneath a flag, before people dressed in a blue uniform, during a Sunday evening gospel service. They have been taught that believers are called to public as well as to private worship: and in public worship too, as the swearing-in ceremony makes clear, The Salvation Army has its own traditions.

Their Way in Worship

The history of Christian worship has been a long duel between form and freedom.

It looks as if the earliest Church was free and easy in its worship, at least if the state of affairs at Corinth is anything to go by: 'When you meet for worship, one man has a hymn, another a teaching, another a revelation from God, another a message in strange tongues, and still another an explanation of what is said. Everything must be of help to the church . . . two or three at most should speak, one after the other . . . God has not called us to be disorderly, but peaceful' (1 Corinthians 14, *Today's English Version*).

Here we see one perennial problem for those who lead Christian worship: how to bring order out of enthusiasm. 'If . . . someone starts speaking in strange tongues . . . if some ordinary people or unbelievers come in, won't they say that you are crazy?' Many a minister since Paul's day has faced quite the opposite problem: how to liven up a production that seems totally dead and devoid of audience participation.

And for all we know, it may have been like that in the first century too. All attempts to deduce the precise form of worship favoured by the early Christians are bound to fail, first for lack of evidence, and secondly because there is no reason to suppose that the early Christians were precise in matters of worship anyway. The cosmopolitan group at Corinth would naturally favour an improvised, do-it-yourself approach, but believers brought up in the traditions of the Jewish synagogue were already familiar with the advantages of working from a script.

And that script, as it came down through the centuries, developed into the Anglican Book of Common Prayer. We may presume that the Baptismal Service of 1662 was read over the young William Booth. But the grave eloquence of Thomas Cranmer sounded strange and archaic even then. The incomparable language of the Prayer Book may appeal to the thoughtful and aesthetically sensitive mind even in the twentieth century, but back in the nineteenth, it appealed to the young pawnbroker's apprentice not at all.

'The English national church of eighty years ago had reached a depth of cold formality and uselessness that can hardly be imagined today . . . even when an earnest clergyman came to any church, he had really to battle against great prejudices on both sides if he wished to make any of the "common people" welcome at "common prayer . . ." the way the appointed services were gone through was only too often such as to make everyone look on the whole matter as one which only concerned the clergy.'

This was the judgment of George Scott Railton, first Salvation Army Commissioner, and opponent of Anglicanism as much on social as religious grounds. The young William Booth, he informs us, found a home in Methodism, where 'the services were, to some extent, independent of books, earnest preaching of the truth was often heard from the pulpits, and some degree of real concern for the spiritual advancement of the people was manifested by the preachers'.

The young Booth had joined the Wesleyans, most conservative of the Methodist groups, to whom, it will be noted, Railton awards only half marks. Their worship was still in partial bondage to books, for they had retained the Anglican matins while replacing evensong with a preaching service. But the future General found it as hard to stay inside the chapel as to sit through worship in church. He cared little for formal worship of any kind. 'Truly I thought then that there was one God, and that John Wesley was His prophet, and that the Methodists were His special people. The church was, I believe, one thousand members strong . . . however, I had time for but few of their great gatherings, having chosen the Meadow Platts as my parish, because my heart went out after the poorest of the poor. I have lived, thank God, to witness the separation between layman and cleric become more and more obscured, and to see Jesus Christ's idea of changing in a moment ignorant fishermen into fishers of men nearer and nearer realization.'

For the young man who fished for souls on Meadow Platts, the essential ingredients of worship were prayer, preaching, personal testimony, Scripture reading and song, made meaningful by personal concern and compassion for those involved. Thus did he minister to a girl dying of consumption: 'Having . . . sung hymns of triumph round her bed as her spirit took its passage to the skies, . . . we brought the coffin out into the street, and urged the few neighbours who stood shivering by, to prepare for their dying day. We then processioned to the cholera burial ground . . . obtaining permission from the chaplain to hold another little meeting by the graveside, after he had read the ordinary service. . . .'

Clearly the 'ordinary service' was as meaningless to the young Booth as was the mass to John Knox. The Army's worship, like that of the radical Methodism from which it sprang, would come to centre on preaching; but not on the long and well-prepared sermon of the Calvinist tradition. Even as you set out for the cholera burial ground, you urge the neighbours to be prepared. The important thing is to get people converted.

In the revivalist tradition, matins soon went the way of evensong. Out on the frontier of the American west, in the great 'camp meetings', the work of winning souls could be very exciting indeed. And here originated such 'typically Salvationist' features as the repeated singing of choruses, the appeal for souls to come forward and be converted, the conducting of the singing by the leader who stands on a platform and not in a pulpit. Back to first-century Corinth? William Booth and his wife Catherine certainly thought so.

'Hayle; Cornwall: Monday evening; chapel crowded. Nearly all the congregation stayed to the prayer meeting that followed, and many appeared deeply affected. A strong prejudice prevails here against inviting anxious enquirers to any part of the building. I . . . considering the crowded state of the chapel, . . . determined to try it . . . I gave a short address, and again invited those who wished to decide for Christ to come forward. After waiting for a minute or two, the solemn silence was broken by the cries of a woman who at once left her pew . . . and fell down at the Mercy Seat . . . a scene ensued beyond description. The cries and groans were piercing in the extreme; and when the stricken souls apprehended Jesus as their Saviour, the shouts of praise and thanksgiving were in proportion to the previous sorrow.'

Here, still in William Booth's Methodist period, is the scenario for future Salvation Army worship. The formal framework is provided by hymns and Bible reading, the sermon is short and sharp, and the action that follows the word is not the breaking of the bread, not the elevation of the host, but the movement of penitent souls to the Mercy Seat. That Mercy Seat—or Penitent-form—was to develop from a row of chairs in a mission hall to become, by the 1930s—a varnished bench adorned with texts and fenced off with ropes. In recent years simpler Penitent-forms have returned. In the Congo ropes were removed because it was believed that no witch could touch them and survive.

Thus the pattern of Salvationist worship was set by the preaching service of nineteenth-century revivalism. The one thing you had to avoid was 'churchiness'. For the church was felt to be a middle-class, formal, snobbish affair, while the mission was a working-class, lively and loving concern. 'The great missionary movement of the non-Roman churches grew up', writes Lesslie Newbigin in *One Body, one Gospel, one World* 'at a time when those churches were largely blind to the missionary implications of churchmanship. There was no way in which those who were obedient to the Great Commission could express their obedience except by forming separate organizations for the purpose.' The association of church with privilege and indifference goes far to explain the Army's adoption of military terminology, and the oft-repeated heart cry of the Army's sixth General—Albert Orsborn. 'We are not a church—we are a permanent mission to the un-converted.' Here too is the reason for some of the Army's odd vocabulary, so baffling to outsiders, whereby the choir is called the songster brigade and the Sunday school teacher is a company guard. Most of these fine distinctions are lost when you translate them into the languages of Africa and Asia, though some eager spirits have tried to preserve them.

A sympathetic account of Salvationist worship in the early 1880s was given by *The Indian Witness*. 'The leader announces a hymn, and reads and expounds it verse by verse in the order of singing' (this is 'lining out'—originally, it seems, for the benefit of illiterates, and latterly a delusion to those who are tempted to waffle). 'While

singing the last verse of a hymn the leader may be seen
getting down on his knees, and his example is followed
by the people who are still singing . . . as soon as the last
word of song is finished the voice of prayer is heard. . . .
There may be a little talk, or bits of talk before the singing
is resumed, but generally after singing one or more hymns,
a brief Bible lesson is read and expounded. While one
Captain speaks the other interrupts him freely, and con-
ventional stiffness is at an immense discount. . . . Probably
the meeting may be thrown open and the audience invited
to testify or exhort as inclined—after an hour or more the
Captain . . . gives an address preparatory to an invitation
to seekers to come forward for prayers. He invites peni-
tents to come and kneel at the communion railing and pray
while all the rest are praying. . . . When he concludes he
simply pronounces the ordinary benediction and the service is at an end. From first to last all is informal.'

The Indian Witness concluded with a comment that
ought to gladden the heart of any Salvationist anywhere.
'The best thing about a Salvationist meeting is the hopeful
tender feeling that pervades it. They do not preach or
exhibit a sour godliness. They joy and rejoice in God,
and their joy is natural. . . .'

And what of the Army's alleged irreverence? On this
The Statesman and Friend of India acutely remarked:
'The apparent familiarity, the free and easiness, with
which these men address the Deity, appears, . . . to result
from their extraordinarily vivid realization of His continued presence. . . . The Salvationists . . . never enter
His presence because they never quit it. . . . Without any
ceremonial preparation they break out in prayer as in the
ordinary language of conversation, and with as little
ceremony they break off and address the audience.
Matthew Arnold speaks of the dissenter addressing God
as if He were a man in the next house. The Salvationist

addresses God as if He were a man at his elbow.'

Such was the ideal of early Salvationist worship: such is the ideal still, as those who have shared in it will know. But if informality and spontaneity was the great virtue, then subjectivity was the great temptation. Did you go to the meeting to 'get a blessing' or to worship God? William Booth's followers would have considered the question a foolish quibble, for what better worship could one offer than the scene in which souls surrender at the Mercy Seat? Their song book (not of course, a 'hymn book') was divided into sections reminiscent of *Wesley's Hymns*: After the Founder's song ('O boundless salvation'—the Movement's anthem) came The Suffering Saviour—Sinners Invited—Sinners Warned—Death—Judgment—Hell. Only in 1953 did the new Song Book appear, beginning with 'God'. And of the 27 songs or hymns devoted to 'God, His Being and His praise' and 'His Works', only one could be claimed for a Salvationist author. This is an anonymous ballad from Christian Mission days:

> Praise God for what He's done for me,
> Once I was blind, but now I see. . . .

The subjective strain is obvious once more: God is to be praised, not for what He is, but for what He has done 'for me'; and the true home of the song, like many Army compositions, is in the 'experience and testimony' section.

Disillusion with traditional liturgy and form, plus the urgency of the revivalist tradition, helps to explain the ease with which the Army abandoned the traditional sacraments of baptism and Holy Communion. The East London Christian Missioners, with their Methodist background, practised infant baptism. 'I have', declared Bramwell Booth, in some cases sprinkled as many as thirty in one service. . . . We had a simple yet very definite formula whereby the parents engaged to give the children over to God to be the servants of God and train them for Him. This practice died down very gradually, chiefly because there was no very strong conviction behind it. . . .'

So much for Saint Augustine, who held that infants who died without baptism must pass to everlasting fire! The Christian Missioners thought more generously of the hereafter, and having dropped the baptism of babies, might perhaps have been expected to try believers' baptism instead. But nobody, it seems, thought of this. In the early 1880s, when so many 'army' customs first germinated, the converts who flooded the new movement were concerned to create their own rites, their own ceremonies, their own religious culture. At first uniforms were anything but uniform. Railton had a tin label, with the words 'Salvation Army' stamped into it. This he affixed to T. Henry Howard's bowler hat. Evangelist Dowdle—the saved railway guard—wore a splendid plume, and this aroused comment when women seeking holiness had their ostrich feathers clipped from their hats as they knelt at the Penitent-form. Clearly Dowdle wore his plume for the Lord's glory, and not his own. But standardization was on the way in: yellow, red and blue ribbon appeared in 1881, and in 1883 the General issued an order stressing 'the greatly increased value of uniform with every fresh growth of the Army's publicity . . . how important for every soldier to make a public demonstration every time he crosses the threshold'.

And in February 1882 the *Nonconformist and Independent* announced that for the first time in church history, the Holy Communion had been administered by a woman. Would this be yet another 'first' for the Army? Would it prove a historic precedent? Quite the contrary, for as the flag, the crest and the uniform came in, the Holy Communion was on its way out.

Chief theoreticians of the move were Catherine Booth
and the long under-estimated Railton. He it was who saw
the new movement as a revival of the seventeenth-
century Quakers. George Fox and 'his Salvation Army
two hundred years ago' had been the first to dispense
with sacraments and had provided—in Robert Barclay's
Apology for the True Christian Divinity (1678) arguments
as convincing—or as unconvincing—as most of the others
put forward in the long debate about what Christ did or
did not intend His followers to do. Railton being persuaded, Catherine Booth followed. In one of her great
addresses at Exeter Hall in London she declared: 'Another
mock salvation is presented in the form of *ceremonies and
sacraments* . . . men are taught that by going through them
or partaking of them . . . they are to be saved . . . what an
inveterate tendency there is in the human heart to trust
in outward forms, instead of seeking the inward grace!'

Her husband was a utilitarian. Converted drunkards
might fall foul of fermented communion wine, male
chauvinists might object to women celebrants—but to
abandon women evangelists would be unthinkable.
Dissension might break out over who might participate
and who might not. The final decision was announced in
the *War Cry* on 2 January 1883—and it was all tied up
with the nineteenth-century distinction between a 'church'
and a 'mission'. William Booth stated:

'In the north of England . . . a clergyman said . . . that
it is evident that The Salvation Army is not a church. To
be a church there must evidently be the exercise of sacra-
mental functions, which evidently are not duly appreciated
by the Army. We are . . . getting away from the ordinary
idea of a church every day. It seems as if a voice from
heaven had said that we are to be an army, separate from,
going before, coming after, and all round about the
existing churches.

'But we are asked by the churches, what should be our attitude to you? We answer: "What is your attitude towards the Fire Brigade? Or . . . towards the Lifeboat Crew?"

'. . . Now if the sacraments are not conditions of salvation, and if the introduction of them would create division of opinion and heart burning, and if we are not professing to be a church, nor aiming at being one, but simply a force for aggressive salvation purposes, is it not wise for us to postpone any settlement of the question, to leave it over for some future day, when we shall have more light? . . .'

'Meanwhile we do not prohibit our own people . . . from taking the sacraments. We say "If this is a matter of your conscience, by all means break bread. The churches and chapels around you will welcome you for this, but in our own ranks . . . let us mind our own business. Let us remember His love every hour of our lives, . . . and let us eat His flesh and drink His blood continually. . . . And further, there is one baptism on which we are all agreed . . and that is the baptism of the Holy Ghost. . . ."

'We are bringing out a formal service for the dedication of children. . . . By this soldiers can introduce their children to the army. Before this is gone through . . . you must explain to the parents that unless they are willing to bring up their children as soldiers and officers in the army they cannot have any part of it. . . .'

Were there waverers, even after this? Bramwell Booth, the Army's second General, claimed to have been a reluctant convert. He administered Holy Communion, he declared, for some time after the rest had stopped; but he did not mention when or where he stopped himself.

There is no doubt that when The Salvation Army gave up baptism and the Lord's Supper, it joined the Society of Friends out on an ecclesiastical limb. 'Why does The

Salvation Army not add water when performing their baptism?' asks a bewildered Sergeant P. N. Okoli in the Nigeria/Ghana edition of the *War Cry*. He is not the first—or the last—to be puzzled.

No doubt a few people moved from the Army to other churches over the question. No statistics exist, but they do not seem to be many. Few Salvationists outside parts of Lutheran Scandinavia make a practice of receiving Holy Communion regularly at church; for to the born and bred Salvationist, the sacraments of baptism and the Lord's Supper are simply not part of his religious scenery. Generations have now been born, lived and died according to the Army's rites, and the language of the dedication service is now venerable with age and hallowed by the profoundest sentiments of love and loyalty.

'You must not keep her back from hardship, suffering, poverty or sacrifice in the service of Jesus Christ . . . as far as you can you must keep from her all intoxicating drink, tobacco, harmful reading and every other influence which may injure her in mind or body. . . . If you are willing to make these promises, I will receive the child in the name of God and of The Salvation Army.'

It is just the same with other symbols too: the flag—red for the blood of Christ, yellow for the fire of the Holy Spirit, blue for purity—placed on the coffin of the Salvationist promoted to Glory; the sound of a brass band, the teenager in uniform for the first time, the informal delight in God which characterizes Army worship at its best—all these are evocative symbols that convey the mystery of God's presence. For sacraments are above all drama, and the Army, finding little meaning in the old classics, has sought to invent new dramas of its own. But like other Christians, Salvationists who find their own symbols profoundly meaningful do not always remember that to the uninitiated they may appear odd, alien, or downright daft.

It has been claimed that the Army's non-observance of the sacraments is a positive witness, a prophetic declaration of the truth that no outward rite is needed to put a man right with his Maker. And so indeed it is, for the benefit of any benighted high churchmen who contend that Pope, or Bishop, or water baptism are compulsory conditions of Christian living. But the witness of Quaker and Salvationist on the sacraments is essentially a witness to the Church, and not to the world. It is well to point out that water baptism alone will not put a man right with God—but how much impact does this make on a generation that doubts if God exists at all?

No concerted move has ever been made to reintroduce the traditional sacraments into the Army. Given the Movement's constitution and structure, it is hard to see how such an attempt could succeed. Among the Ibibio people of Cross River State in Nigeria Salvationists hold quarterly Love Feasts—in which on at least one occasion pepsi-cola was drunk and Christ's words 'do this in remembrance of Me' were referred to if not recited. A Methodist couple had their child baptized with water by a Salvation Army officer in Gibraltar . . . but these are marginal events, and within the Army as a whole there is little opportunity to form pressure groups; nor does it appear that any article proposing reintroduction of the sacraments has ever appeared in any Army publication. Any attempt to do so would have to begin unofficially, locally and without publicity—and even then it might arouse the dissension that William Booth feared in 1882. For most Salvationists seem satisfied with the ceremonies they have already.

The Army meeting is, in its way, as much a set form of worship as the canon of the mass. The 'five-hymn sandwich' of the English free churches is its first cousin' and if the Army version is often somewhat less tedious, it is often because there is more variety of filling in the sandwich and because more than one chef takes part in its preparation. The style of music may well vary from country to country, but in the West at least it is likely that the level of the music will be higher than that of the speech. The songsters may sing rather well, the Bible may be read rather badly. The sermon will at least be delivered in a colloquial and not a parsonical tone of voice; and the days have long passed when the Norwegian Carl Breien was criticized for using sermon notes: 'even to quote Bible texts . . was not considered "real Army" '.

Informal, unscripted worship requires of course, even more care and preparation than the Prayer Book variety, and as an example of what it can deteriorate into we may take the scene observed by ex-Commissioner A. M. Nicol in London in 1910. What happens when the Penitent-form is no longer thronged week by week? When few newcomers darken the doors of the hall? According to Nicol, this: 'When the preliminaries were over the Captain, in a strident voice, as if the heart had been beaten out of him and he had to make up for the lack of natural feeling by the extent of his vocal power, announced that the meeting would be thrown open for testimony . . . no one seemed inclined to get up . . . a song was sung from the *Social Gazette* newspaper . . . and the Captain stated . . . "Last week I had to pay five shillings loss on the newspaper account. For pity's sake buy them up." A woman got up and screamed a testimony about the lack of the Holy Ghost and the spirit of backbiting. Two young men walked out, and several soldiers in uniform whispered to each other. The Salvation Army throughout England and Scotland has ceased to be true to itself.'

Poor Nicol's sweeping generalization was sadly over-done, but he made his observation during the 'second generation', when the Army had to learn, like so many groups of Christian enthusiasts before it, that freedom in worship means freedom to sink as well as to rise, and that the clichés of a third-rate mind can be as boring as the Prayer Book you cannot find the place in.

Nicol thought that reluctance to spring up and testify was 'a sure sign that the Army was no longer true to itself'. But he may well have been wrong. It may also have indicated that a better-educated generation preferred to think before it opened its mouth. The participation of the ordinary wayfaring Christian in praise, prayer and witness remains one of the most precious elements in Army worship, and yet even among Salvationists the temptation to leave it all to the professionals is not unknown. In Africa a 'grand amen' still punctuates and rounds off each prayer, but in the West the people of God can scarcely raise a mumble. Spontaneous and unregimented kneeling, standing, and moving can give place, with the passing of the years and enthusiasms, to long and soporific sitting. Salvationists do not stand to recite the Apostles' Creed—for they do not recite creeds—and in some of their meetings the people hardly stand up at all. They have never felt the need for holy hush before and after public worship, for like their Jewish brethren they feel no doubt that the voice of the Lord is heard in chatter as well as in silence. But friendly chatter can—alas—deteriorate into thoughtless hubbub.

Moreover, Salvationists in their public worship have not always noted the difference drawn by wise old Isaac Watts between free and extempore prayer. The former is 'done by some work of meditation before we begin to speak in prayer' while in the latter 'we without any reflection or meditation beforehand address ourselves to

God and speak the thoughts of our hearts as fast as we conceive them'. As Stephen Winward rightly notes, the latter is, 'except in the case of highly gifted individuals ... no more effective than unprepared preaching'. In the Army the place of set prayers—collects and the like—has always been taken by the singing of choruses and refrains. These vary in quality from the sublime to the ridiculous. But most public prayer remains free—indeed extempore—and the wish of many Salvationists would seem to be for a worship that combines teaching with the traditional cheerful features of the 'old Army' meeting.

Thus the long duel between form and freedom continues—and it is likely to continue to do so as long as men pray and praise, for it reflects the permanent problem of keeping a balance between the objective and subjective sides of worship—between God in Himself on one hand and man in his need on the other. Army worship certainly varies greatly from country to country. In Korea few wear uniform, while in parts of Britain the visitor in civvies may feel like a man in jeans at the Rotary Club. Music may be of the brass band and songster variety—or it may feature African anthems laboriously written out on paper detached from a school exercise book. But there is indeed a Highest Common Factor—the Lord of Glory—and the Army meeting remains at heart a simple preaching service in the Protestant tradition, allowing for audience participation both in prayer and witness. Here it can certainly teach the rest of the Church a thing or two. 'One of the qualities in short supply' (at the World Council of Churches Assembly) 'in Nairobi', writes Commissioner Harry Williams, was 'sheer joy in the Lord . . . spontaneous fullthroated singing'. Even the right to pray in your own words has to be fought for at times. On one occasion at the Ecumenical Institute, Bossey, Switzerland, the various church traditions offered selections from their prayers and praises: those who planned to improvise were left with almost no time to do it in. And this in the land where members of the Reformed Churches address their Maker in correct High German, while Salvationists assume that He understands the broadest Swiss!

Thoughtful Salvationists have, of course, been touched by the psychological revolution in their worship as well as in their faith. Back in 1930 the *Staff Review* asked 'Is prayer autosuggestion?' and added that 'from psychology has come one of the most subtle and plausible forms of modern attacks upon religious teaching and experience . . . intelligent young men and women . . . imagine that psychology can account for religious experience on a purely subjective and naturalistic basis'.

The Editor failed to notice, apparently, that back in 1922 the sympathetic R. S. Thouless had studied some of the Army's classical methods from the psychological point of view: 'At the end of the . . . Salvation Army service . . . people were invited to come up to the Mercy Seat on the stage . . . to seek consecration. One of the leaders was repeating in confident and slightly monotonous tones: "Jesus calls you. Come. Come. Come now." The congregation were asked to bow their head and sing with eyes closed. The closed eyes, the monotonous singing and the repetition of the word "Come" on the stage, all combined to produce in the audience a state verging on the hypnoidal. The same verse was being sung over and over again by the congregation. . . . It contained some such words as "I give myself to Jesus" . . . it succeeded in breaking down the resistance of several of the congregation to the act of . . . stepping on to the stage. . . .'

And in those days they had no public address systems! There would seem to be a generation gap in the Army, at least in Britain, over the old-style prayer meeting. Some older officers continue to revel in them while the younger generation resents 'being kept singing, singing the same chorus for over an hour!'

'On the whole', wrote *The Indian Witness* nearly a century ago, 'a meeting of the Salvationists is very enjoyable to anyone who can in a moderate degree enter into sympathy with the leaders and their purpose.' That kind comment is still true today—provided those Salvationists who lead in worship are sure what their purpose is and adapt their approach to the needs of their people.

CHAPTER SIX

Their Social Conscience

In signing their *Articles of War* our recruits have promised to strive both for the 'present welfare' and the 'eternal salvation' of their fellow-men. Many of these, we may suspect, are more interested in the former than the latter. Indeed, the Army is often mistaken for a charitable voluntary society like Oxfam or even the Red Cross: the Movement's own publicity does not always discourage this misunderstanding.

Salvationists have always protested that they find no conflict between the call to love God and the duty to serve their neighbour. 'The germ of the welfare services of The Salvation Army', wrote General Frederick Coutts, 'may be seen in the action of the teenage William Booth who with his friend, Will Sansom, provided for a Nottingham beggar woman who shuffled about the streets and slept in doorways. The two lads collected money from their friends, found a little cabin which they furnished, and made a simple home for her!' For the Christian, charity begins in God. 'How could I hope', cries an anonymous voice from the early days of the Christian Mission, 'to impart any spiritual help if I could not do something to alleviate the dreadful poverty? Would they not call it a mockery to talk about their souls when their bodies were perishing with hunger?'

The Salvation Army's organized social work began, not in East London, but in Australia—and General Coutts notes that this is hardly surprising, for 'the first Army meeting to be held in that continent concluded with an invitation by John Gore to his own house and table to any listener who lacked a square meal'. This practical attitude led to the establishment of a home for ex-prisoners in Melbourne on 8 December 1883. It earned the approval of the Chief Commissioner of Police, who declared that 'the Prison Gate Brigade succeeds in reaching a large class of unfortunates whose . . . depravity defies ordinary measures'. Sensation was caused—and some public good-will lost for a while, when the unfortunates appeared on the streets of Melbourne dressed in government surplus red tunics, formerly worn by soldiers of the Queen.

Nearly a century later we find Major Bernard Smith pioneering a rehabilitation project for alcoholics in Costa Rica. He makes no attempt to put Costa Rican unfortu-nates into red tunics, but he does insist on maintaining good order and discipline. 'People don't like the word "Army" and what it implies', he declares, 'but we run this com-munity with unbreakable rules and we reward good behaviour.' Moreover, he makes the religious basis of his work clear to all who turn up, offering 'a religious service which is as ecumenical as possible but emphasizes that there does exist a supreme Power on whom lost and desperate people can rely'.

So the Salvationist's concern for man's present welfare is intended to be an expression of Christ's love. Social action and love for souls are—or ought to be—but two sides of the same coin. Yet nowadays, at least in many countries of the West, the Army is often regarded as a social welfare organization rather than as a religious body Professor Richard Hoggart summed it up neatly in *The Uses of Literacy*. Noting that the English working classes, while largely indifferent to the Churches, lacked that militant hostility to religion found in 'anticlerical' countries he continued: 'The Salvation Army is widely regarded as

Artist's impression of an early-day open-air meeting.

From its beginnings the Army has sought to reach the masses with the Gospel. Such vehicles as this, originally called forts (later batteries) went out on evangelical missions.

With East-enders in the City. A young people's band marching during the thirties.

With East-enders in the hopfields of Kent during the forties. Goodwill officers serving tea to the thirsty.

Salvation Army Articles of War. These five young people having signed them,
were recently sworn-in as Salvation Army soldiers. By this act, they accepted
Salvation Army doctrines and pledged themselves to faithful service under the
flag of the Army saying: 'I do here and now call upon all present to witness that
I have entered into this undertaking and signed these "Articles of War" of my
own free will, feeling that the love of Christ, who died to save me, requires from
me this devotion of my life to His service for the salvation of the whole world,
and therefore do here declare my full determination, by God's help, to be a true
soldier of The Salvation Army till I die.'

PROTECTION OF **YOUNG GIRLS**

TUESDAY MORNING, JULY 12

AT ELEVEN O'CLOCK,

PRINCE'S HALL, PICCADILLY

ADDRESSES BY

MRS. BOOTH.

Mrs. JOSEPHINE BUTLER

Professor Stuart, M.P.

PERCY BUNTING, ESQ.,

Sir Baldwyn Leighton, M.P.,

F. A. BEN

AND OTHE

CHAIR TO BE

SAMUEL MORL

A few Reserved Seats at c

Pioneer social work. From its earliest days the Army has been concerned to obey its Founder's command 'Go and *Do* something' about social evils.

Early-day persecution. Striking evidence of the steps taken to oppose the Army's open-air evangelism.

TO THE INHABITANTS OF THE
CITY OF SALISBURY

FELLOW CITIZENS,

We have endured for a considerable time the noise and nuisance caused a created by the proceedings of THE SALVATION ARMY, through their peram bulating the Streets of our City, notwithstanding which we have patiently ke from resorting to any measures of opposition in the earnest hope that the governi body of this City, would in accord with the popular desire. PUT A STO TO THE NUISANCE thus created; but that patience has been exercise in vain; the governing body of this city have failed to move in the matter, an will not yet put in force the power which they possess FOR THE STOPPIN OF THIS NUISANCE!!! We therefore wish it to be known that a Society h been formed for the purpose of doing what the executive fail to do. Their so object will be

To STOP the Parading of the Streets by th
SALVATION ARMY.

They will employ various ways and means with which to accomplish this en They will cause to be forcibly broken the ranks of the Salvation Army when Procession through the Streets, and they will use every means in their pow TO STOP AND RESIST THOSE PROCESSIONS FROM SO DOING. the same time they will give such advice and instructions to those whom th may employ, or those whose sympathy and help they enlist, to have due respe for their persons, especially more so those of the weaker sex. But althoug they will so advise them, they will not be responsible for what may arise, shou they be first assulted. This Society will also assist any one or more (should the become involved in any difficulty through their exertions on their behalf), both pecuniari and by other means, so as that they be not wrongfully used. This Society will not in any w countenance any difficulty which any one or more may bring to his or themselves INSID OF THE SALVATION PLACE OF WORSHIP, which this Society thinks both a FI AND PROPER PLACE FOR THEM TO KEEP TO. This Society therefore ca upon all those Citizens who are able to assist them in any way so to do, and by combini together and FORCING THE SALVATIONISTS to do what the Executive are so loth to TO BRING BACK THAT PEACEABLE & QUIET STATE OF THIS CIT WHICH PREVIOUS TO THE EXISTENCE OF THIS NUISANCE, WA

A PATTERN TO THE NATION.

Given under our hands this 18th day of February, 1881,

FREDERICK RODWAY, Chairma
SAM   HOWE, Secretary

Indonesian Salvationists trekking to a meeting. They often journey many miles for this purpose.

Up-to-date techniques. A radio telephone maintains links between mission stations.

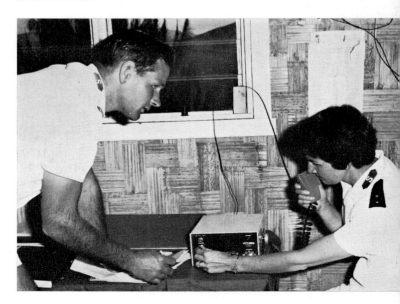

In the Harari township corps, Salisbury, Rhodesia, the wife of the Commanding Officer ministers to the needy.

A convert is made in East Africa. A penitent kneeling at the improvised Mercy Seat (the Army drum) is counselled.

'Where there is need, there is The Salvation Army'. Service during the Second World War.

Work in New Guinea began in 1956. Commissioner (later General) Frederick Coutts commissions the first national officer.

Like other missionary societies the Army was compelled to withdraw from the mainland of China but still maintains work among the Chinese people of Hong Kong and Taiwan.

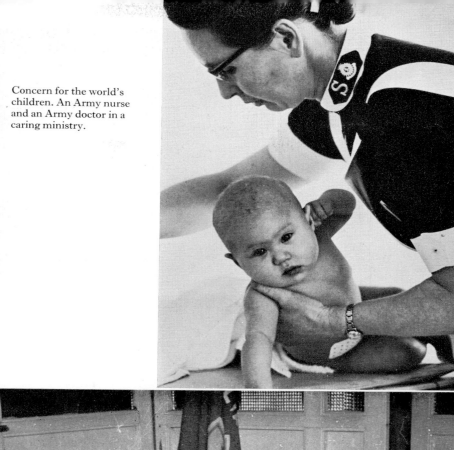

Concern for the world's children. An Army nurse and an Army doctor in a caring ministry.

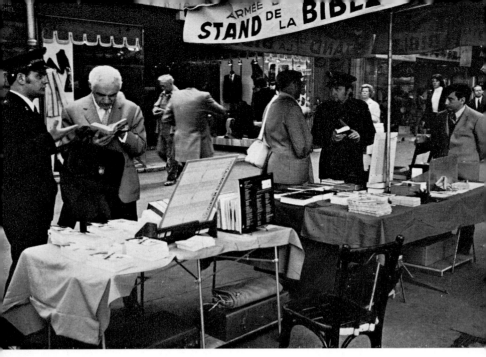

The eldest daughter of William and Catherine Booth conducted the Army's first meeting in Paris in 1881. Here Salvation Army officers of today continue the work.

Goodwill officers in Sweden who proudly preserve the title 'Slum' on their uniform hats.

Those who belong to no one belong to us! This was the belief of the Army's Founder. Salvationists carry it out as here in Bangladesh.

A new member of the Home League (the Army's Women's Meeting) receives her badge in Kenya.

The Salvation Army began work in the United States of America in 1880. A young Salvationist assists with the placing of a wreath at the spot where Commissioner George Scott Railton and the pioneer party landed.

Ambulance and equipment provided for the Booth Memorial Medical Center, New York.

Midnight patrol in Glasgow.

Lieut.-Colonel Richard Williams, author of *Missing*, a best selling book about the Army's work among missing persons, is seen interviewing a wife.

Somebody loves me!

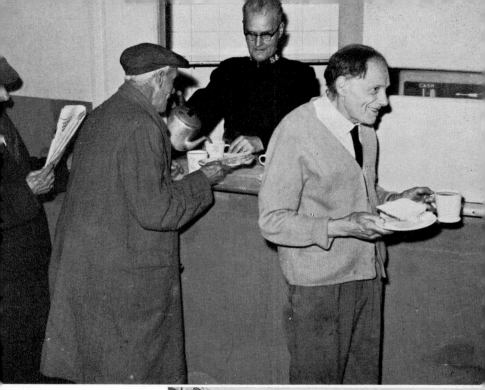

Soup, soap and salvation!
'You cannot preach to
people with empty
stomachs,' said William
Booth. Care for the
physical needs of the
destitute is a priority with
Salvationists.

Booth House, Whitechapel
Road, London. Here, close
to Mile End Waste where
William Booth began his
work is the Army's most
up-to-date Men's Social
Service Centre comprising
Alcoholics Treatment
Centre, Men's Shelter and
a Bail Hostel for men on
remand from the Courts.

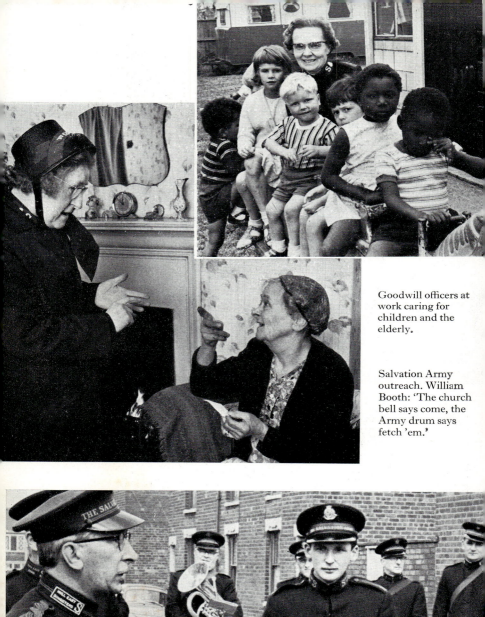

Goodwill officers at
work caring for
children and the
elderly.

Salvation Army
outreach. William
Booth: 'The church
bell says come, the
Army drum says
fetch 'em.'

a refuge for the slightly dotty, but it "does a good work" and is respected for that. The *War Cry* still sells in the pubs.'

The Army was born amid the great outburst of Victorian philanthropy and voluntary effort that prepared the way for the modern welfare state. Dr Barnardo cared for homeless children, Josephine Butler championed fallen women, William Booth declared that the London poor should be treated at least as well as a cab horse which had shelter, food and work, . . . and the motive for all these good deeds was profoundly religious. The pioneer Salvationists were concerned with the salvation of souls before they considered the nurture of bodies. They undertook the latter because, not being humbugs, they perceived that it was a natural expression of the former. But they deplored 'coal and blanket' evangelism, and regarded social action for its own sake with as great a suspicion as cultural activity. 'Do the hotchpotch mixtures of Christ and Shakespeare, Paul and Dickens . . . serve to bring the people to Christ?' This was the heart cry of Catherine Booth. And her husband William declared: 'Legislation will do much to counteract the mischief of pauperism, but the spread of religious feelings will do more. The true Christian is a real self-helper. In bringing the truths of religion before the suffering masses we are also assisting in the great work of social reform. When we have taught people to be religious, half the battle has been won.'

In taking up the cause of social reform, the Army was—and still is—careful to avoid party political involvement: a distinction easier to draw in theory than in practice! Yet in earlier days, when the Movement had little or nothing to lose, it was not unwilling to stand and be counted on questions where social and political interest coincided.

In 1885 Bramwell Booth, with the journalist W. T.

Stead and others, stood in the dock at Bow Street charged with the illegal abduction of Eliza Armstrong, aged thirteen.

Prior to 1875, the child over the age of twelve was regarded by English law as a consenting adult in sexual intercourse. In that year the age of consent was raised to thirteen, but in 1885 W. T. Stead of the *Pall Mall Gazette* launched a campaign to prove that child prostitution was widespread. In order to show what the public was reluctant to believe, Stead 'bought' Eliza for £5. She was cared for by the Army, taken over to France—and later found herself a key witness at Bow Street. For Stead's sensational articles on *The Maiden Tribute of Modern Babylon*, which led to a change in the law, also brought its author to the dock. A monster petition with 340,000 signatures was deposited on the floor of the House of Commons by eight uniformed Salvationists, and the age of consent was raised to sixteen. Stead got six months in jail, Bramwell Booth was acquitted, and Rebecca Jarrett— the converted prostitute who had arranged the 'sale' of Eliza—got six months as well. She, if anyone, was the victim of earnest reformers who held that the end justified the means—at least some means. But she lived to write, in a happy old age, 'how good Jesus is to a poor, lost, degraded woman'. The turning point came, not when the Army preached to Rebecca, but when Captain 'Hawker' Jones—a girl of nineteen—tried to nurse her back to health. 'They do it all for nothing' Rebecca kept exclaiming.

Another venture of early days led to that curiosity of the philumenists' collection—the Salvation Army matchbox label.

LIGHTS IN DARKEST ENGLAND
Security from fire
Fair wages for fair work

'Our mission', declared the matchboxes, 'is for God and humanity.' The older phosphorus matches could be struck anywhere: on a stone, on a wall, on the sole of your shoe—but the price paid for this was the terrible 'phossy jaw'—the necrosis that ate away the bones of the face. 'Safety' matches were invented, not for the safety of those who struck them, but for the health of those who produced them.

William Booth's match factory in Old Ford paid four pence a gross where the larger firms paid only 2½d. The chemistry professor at University College London declared that he used Salvation Army matches and no others. By the end of the nineteenth century safety matches were the rule, and phossy jaw was a thing of the past. One part of the great *Darkest England* scheme had been brought to a successful conclusion.

It would seem that the Army is at its best when confronted by a tangible social evil that it can get its teeth into. When Apollyon appears, in all his fearful panoply, then the Army has been ready to challenge him in any quarter of the globe. Child prostitution was not confined to Victorian London. The infant Japanese Salvation Army faced it too. In 1900 there were only a few hundred Salvationists in the country, and licensed prostitution had been illegal since 1872. But in fact a system of debt bondage kept it going handsomely. Girls were not, strictly speaking, bought—they were simply handed over until loans were repaid; and they were forbidden to leave the licensed quarters without the signature both of the manager and the brothel keeper.

An imperial ordinance did indeed proclaim their right to freedom—but as this was written in classical Japanese, many could not understand it. The pioneer Salvationist Gunpei Yamamuro—whose *Common People's Gospel* was to sell over half a million copies—rendered it into colloquial speech. His wife Kiye—from an old Samurai family —took charge of a girls' home for any who might wish to give up the prostitute's life. After a night of prayer in the Kanda hall, the band of Salvationists marched into the Yoshawara quarter with their drum beating. They failed to beat it on the way back, however, for it had been smashed to pieces by thugs hired by the brothel business. The flag was torn to pieces and several marchers beaten up.

But the Army had the letter of the law as well as public opinion on its side. There could be no doubt that many girls had been forced into prostitution against their will, and within a year over twelve thousand young women abandoned the life. On 2 October 1900 an imperial ordinance declared that any woman who wished to give up prostitution had only to go to the nearest police station and say so. Irrespective of debt, she would be set free.

Clearly the battle against the world's oldest profession would not end so easily. The Army's protest had been a spark to set fire to already combustible material—for public opinion had moved against the old-style enforced prostitution. Equal to the courage of those who faced the thugs was the endurance of Fujio Itoh, who from 1902 to 1923 helped over 900 girls to give up their calling. For the path to the police station was far from easy and on two occasions Itoh was beaten up so badly that he spent weeks in hospital. But he succumbed neither to beating nor to bribery.

One of the paradoxes of The Salvation Army has been that some of its greatest achievements in the field of social action have been undertaken in lands where the ranks are very thin indeed. Nowhere is this truer than in France. The land of Pascal and Voltaire has generally proved stony soil for Anglo-Saxon Protestantism, and even in 1976 the Army numbered but 99 places of worship and 35 institutions. But that did not prevent it, back in the

1920s, from tackling the abomination generally known as Devil's Island.

The convict settlement in French Guiana had been opened during the nineteenth century after the abolition of slavery. This Gallic equivalent of Botany Bay had become world famous during the Dreyfus case, and it was not well known that the notorious Devil's Island was only one of a group ironically known as the 'Iles du salut'—the 'Islands of Salvation'. Moral and spiritual redemption was not assisted by the system of 'doublage' under which an ex-convict was required to remain in the colony for as long again as the term of his sentence. The theory was that he would become a model citizen and colonist.

When the young Charles Péan* arrived, however, in 1931, he found in one camp 'paralytics, disfigured syphilitics . . . and a young man who had been blind for six years. His sentence was twenty years for deserting in the face of the enemy; hearing strange footsteps, he cried "Get me out of here" '.

It was in fact the ex-convicts—the 'liberés'—who suffered the most. An estimated 2,393 of them 'wandered in the bush, none knew where, perhaps to meet death'. Péan could think of only one Bible reading adequate to the situation. He turned to the prophet Ezekiel: 'The Lord . . . set me down in the valley which was full of bones . . . and He said unto me, Son of man, can these bones live? And I answered,—O Lord God, Thou knowest.'

Some of the bones at least were destined to live. In 1933 the Army was accredited by the French government to work in the penal settlement. A hostel was opened for vagrant ex-convicts in Cayenne. 'La Maison de France', wrote Péan, 'was a kind of moral and spiritual clinic . . . a hundred "liberés" were constantly under our care, though

---

* Commissioner Charles Péan later to be leader of the Army's work in France.

our worst enemy was the absence of hope among those who could not see themselves returning to ordinary life again.'

The first men to return to ordinary life reached St Nazaire in February 1936. They were French, Vietnamese, Arab, African . . . one had been 'liberated' in Cayenne for eighteen years already. But ships were still sailing in the opposite direction, and Péan was on board himself when the last of them to carry convicts—the *Martinière*—left St Martin de Ré on 22 November 1938. It looked as if the penal settlement might be brought to an orderly end. But then came the Second World War and the fall of France.

When Péan returned to St Laurent du Maroni, after the war, it happened to be Good Friday. 'I reached the hostel in time for the evening meeting . . . I stayed some moments in the shadows. Some men, sitting in a half-circle, were listening to the Captain bringing them the message of Good Friday. His voice was as warm and eager as when . . . thirteen years ago, we spoke to those men for the first time.' The Captain, Pierre Hausdorff, had been in Guiana, away from occupied France, for nine years.

The ending of the convict settlement—the last of the ex-convicts came home in 1962—was certainly a famous victory in the long war between light and darkness. But even then there were casualties. Jules was an ex-convict looking forward eagerly to repatriation; but Péan and Hausdorff discovered him in other company. They 'were walking through a ward occupied by several lepers who were to be transferred to the leper colony at Lacarouni. "O Major," cried one of them, "Look what has happened to me." The doctor had discovered that he was suffering from a stiff leg, and diagnosed the trouble as leprosy'.

Sceptics sometimes ask whether the need for The Salvation Army's work—by which they probably mean its 'wonderful work' of social welfare—has not been rendered obsolete by the rise of the Welfare State. Such doubting Thomases forget that over most of the world there is still little or no welfare state. The blind still lead the blind, as in biblical days, and the poor man still sits with his begging bowl. Often he is reluctant to surrender it. One disabled man who had his patch near the SA Headquarters in Nigeria declined to attend the cripples' Christmas feast on the grounds that Christmas day was one of the busiest in the year and he could not afford to take time off the job!

Meanwhile, on the other side of the continent, a Nairobi newspaper complained of the hordes of disabled beggars who pestered tourists. It was decided to make a start with the rising generation. Potential beggars could learn to do something better and in 1962 the Army opened *Joytown* at Thika, Kenya. Governments who do not have the resources to keep all their able-bodied children in school rarely find much to spend on the handicapped. Here then is a challenge and an opportunity for the voluntary agency. *Joytown* was opened in November 1962 with 24 disabled children. A great voluntary social service had begun.

In 1976, there were in Kenya an estimated 3,000 blind children, plus 150,000 physically handicapped. Of these the Army cares for about a thousand—415 of the blind and 580 of the lame. Facilities range from workshops to secondary schools. In the national primary school leaving examination, the blind pupils obtain above-average results. One former pupil is now a tutor in a teacher training college, while the lame need sit by their begging bowl no more. 'In Nakuru', says an official report, 'there is a small firm which employs handicapped people for the delicate work of producing flamingo feather ornaments . . . at which they are very successful. . . . It is not necessary for the physically-handicapped person to remain in sheltered employment.'

There is, of course, a world-wide trend in social work; a trend towards government takeover. This may be seen from Guyana—where the State takes over the Boys' Home in Georgetown—to Nigeria where the government nationalizes schools. To face such a prospect can be saddening for people who have given life and energy and love—for will not the wild beasts ravage the vineyard? Will not the secular apostles do half the work for twice the pay? Will they perhaps introduce bribery and corruption? Promote their relatives? Or—as others think—should the Christian be ready to work within the secular framework, bringing his Christian insight and compassion with him?

Salvationists are found in both camps. In addition to the many who work 'for the Army', others see in their secular employment an expression of Christian love. And there seems to be no lack of need for the 'frontier' apostles, for governments, no matter how willing they may be to take over well-established institutions, never seem to find cash or people for the job that requires you to go the extra mile—or the extra two, five, or ten miles.

It seems a long way from the disabled children of East Africa to the dropout teenagers of America. If the former have too little, the latter might be thought to possess too much. Too much money and not enough love? When the Rev. Wayne Smith arrived at North Avenue Presbyterian Church in Atlanta, Georgia, he found that there were plenty of problems for an ecumenical ministry to tackle.

'The Salvation Army . . . were having girls as guests', he told the *Atlanta Journal and Constitution*. 'Many of them were runaways, some as young as nine or ten years old. They would get mad at mommie or daddy and run away from home and come to the big city. Black and white, rich and poor came drifting into this area. . . . The trouble was not just with the young men of the counter-culture who would make the girls their sex objects and get them on dope. There were businessmen in their suits and ties who would cruise up and down the streets, see a little girl evidently lost, stop and pick her up, have sex experience with her and drop her off some place. . . .'

Coping with this iniquity was the Army's Captain Judy Moore. She had problems not only with the kerbcrawlers but also with the bureaucrats: 'The . . . Girls' Lodge had just moved from Eleventh Street down to Myrtle Street but they were having problems with a zoning law that would not permit them to be on Myrtle.'

The answer to this problem was the establishment of *Metanoia* (Greek for 'repentance' or 'change of direction') in an old gabled house which was once the stately home of the President of the Mexican National Railroad. In this building the North Avenue Presbyterian Church was able to provide a community centre for all kinds of groups ranging from *The Bridge*—a 'crisis intervention centre' run by a Catholic Priest—via *Peachtree Alternative School* —'a private school for poor kids'—to The Salvation Army Girls' Lodge once faced with eviction from Myrtle Street. Judy Moore's invitation card advertises 'a free and friendly place to stay', it is not difficult to see why Wayne Smith and the North Avenue Presbyterian church thought her work was worth investing in. 'Judy and I stood here in this pothole and prayed. I'll never forget that. We prayed out loud here in the hot sun. We said "Lord, we don't under-stand this. All we want is space for a girls' lodge and this is too big. Lord, what are You trying to tell us." '

The Lord was, it turned out, trying to tell them to turn the big house into multi-purpose *Metanoia*—and if anyone thinks that the kind of faith that prays out loud in a pothole is naïve, too pietistic, out of touch with the

twentieth century—then a free and friendly talk with
Judy Moore will soon convert him. For the care of runaway girls raises difficult problems of confidentiality. The
Girls' Lodge can take up to twenty-five at a time—though
eight could be the best number to cope with—for a
maximum of three days. Clearly it won't work if the
runaway, the 'pushout', the 'nestleaver' thinks that her
friendly counsellor will report her to mommie or daddy—
but anyone under seventeen counts as a juvenile. Judy
gets by on faith, hope, charity and common sense. She
needs plenty of the last-named. 'Hope is the thing we
want to share—hope that things can be different', she
says. 'We try to offer the girls the feeling of not being
alone any more, that what they say and feel is important.'
No drugs, 11 o'clock bedtime, help with the housework—
and a chance to sort yourself out. Church on Sunday is
encouraged but not compulsory.

After over a hundred years of effort, the Army's world-
wide social work includes 504 hostels for the homeless,
116 centres for alcoholics, 37 general hospitals, 53 maternity hospitals and clinics, 154 eventide homes, 5 institutes
for the blind and 172 children's homes. Persons assisted
during disasters add up, it appears, to 1,603,585 in one
year. . . .

But does the Army ram religion down people's throats?
It has always offered help to anybody and everybody
irrespective of creed. Nobody is forced to sing hymns for
their supper—though some of the souls in need may feel
that it might be a good idea to try.

Nevertheless the Christian motivation of most Salvation
Army work is usually fairly obvious. Sermons are not
normally compulsory, but evening prayers may be hard
to avoid. Voltaire, or David Hume, or Mr Worldly
Wiseman, might feel rather uncomfortable.

But Ganesammal, 'a dwarf with deformities of all the

long bones', feels quite at home. Named after the Hindu elephant God, she recently wrote, unaided, a letter to her parents in distant Bombay. Never having been to school she has learnt dressmaking on a special low table, and reading in eight months as an extra. All this at the vocational centre for handicapped women at Nagercoil, Tamil Nadu, India. The Centre's Report may be allowed to say a last word—if not *the* last word—of the Army's social action in the mid-1970s.

'To keep our pride down' (derived from champion tomatoes and egg plants) 'the bandicoots ate all the tapioca grown from the Archbishop's prize cuttings just as it was ready for harvesting. . . . As for our cows— Visuvasam (Faith), Nambikai (Hope) and Anbu (Love) . . . the last is now a big heifer. A new Jersey cow was called Kirubai (Grace) but it was grace we needed when we found out that despite all precautions we had been cheated in the process. We are now wiser in the ways of cows and cow merchants, but how does a Christian who has been taken in sell such a cow without taking someone else in?'

It seems a far cry from Ganesammal the dwarf and Grace the Jersey cow to the suburban citadel with which our story began. The recruits at Ilford are, by world standards, well fed, well housed and well educated. They return—after a stirring sermon and a rousing hymn—to semi-detached houses in a prosperous part of London. Recruits no longer, but soldiers of The Salvation Army, they may perhaps frame their *Articles of War* and hang them on the living-room wall; more probably, as befits an age reticent in religious matters, they may be rolled up and placed in the bedroom drawer. But what is the future of the Movement to which they have committed their lives? How do the forces stand in the five continents which it has invaded, if not conquered?

We turn to this question in part two.

PART TWO

THE ARMY
WORLD WIDE

CHAPTER SEVEN

In Europe

The Salvation Army is an offshoot of European Christianity in general and of Protestantism in particular. It expanded early—and rapidly—into Western Europe: between 1881 and 1895, it 'opened fire' in France, Sweden, Switzerland, Germany, Denmark, the Netherlands, Finland, Italy and Iceland. The Ilford Citadel keeps close links with brethren on the continent—indeed, its band visited West Germany during the Easter before our recruits were enrolled. In West Germany they have a Salvation Army, but few big bands.

The two world wars stand as landmarks in the Army's European history, and the end of the first led to further advances: 1917—Russia, 1919—Czechoslavakia, 1923—Latvia, 1924—Hungary, 1933—Yugoslavia . . . but where are the East European Salvationists now? Some are still alive and well and living behind the iron curtain, but the Army as an organized body no longer exists there.

In most West European countries the Army has seen rapid expansion followed by consolidation and growth, and since the late 1930s a slow numerical decline. The pattern can be traced in Britain as in Sweden—in the Army and in other churches too. Is this the start of a decline and slow death that inevitably follows as man comes of age and outgrows religion? Believers may repine, and those who sit in the seat of the scornful may rejoice, at the sight of the derelict chapel, the empty gallery, the deserted youth club. But things are not so simple. If industrialization leads inevitably to the numerical decline and fall of Christianity, why has the process not taken place in North America and Australasia?

A glance through the Army's Year Book will show that the Movement has done much better—statistically if not spiritually—in Protestant countries than in traditionally Catholic ones. Thus we find recorded in France 99 places of worship and 35 institutions; in Sweden 1,452 places of worship and 90 institutions; Italy, 36 and 8; Norway, 1,231 and 71; Belgium 12 and 12; the Netherlands 184 and 38. . . . In France the going was always tough: William Booth's daughter Catherine—the 'Marechale'—had to face anti-religious hostility quite foreign to the British working classes: 'The uproar was terrible, but just at the worst the Marechale advanced into the middle of the hall, and standing right in the midst of them pleaded like an apostle . . . an excited audience grinned and hooted . . . about half of them were of revolutionary type. . . . One, with a face full of the devil, hissed in rage inconceivable; baring his arm and holding it aloft he shrieked: 'We will hear you if you will talk to us about anything but Jesus. . . . We hate Him. . . . We will have "liberté" but no "amens". No religion; we have had enough of that . . . we have had enough of Jesus . . . Jesuits!' (*The Salvation War, 1885*.)

Similar if less dramatic happenings took place elsewhere. It required much courage and determination to associate oneself with The Salvation Army in its early days. In Berlin the Gauntlett family would find itself surrounded by a crowd at a tram stop.

'Who are they?'
'They must be English.'
'No, look at their hats. It says "Die Heilsarmee".'
'What kind of people are they?'
'The lowest of the low, I am told.'

'But this family looks respectable enough.'
'Then the father must be an eccentric.'

On this dialogue, F. L. Coutts commented: 'Eccentric . . . they were, but not as the world understands eccentricity. They were eccentric in so far as their lives pivoted on an unseen axis. The centre of their lives was the redemptive purpose of God. Why else should Sydney bring his young family to an alien land, wrestle with the grammar of an alien tongue, and pour out his heart over a handful of people in a cattle loft . . . with such intensity that the congregation forgot the lowing of the beasts below them?' (*Portrait of a Salvationist*, by F. L. Coutts, p. 9.)

Similar apostolic deeds were done in other parts of Europe. In Sweden the Army was headed by a woman, Hanna Ouchterlony, commissioned in London's Exeter Hall in 1882. Odd restrictions were devised to make life difficult for the Army—for example: no meetings after sunset. But when precisely was a Swedish sunset? Was it still daytime—so lawyers learnedly debated—if you could read a newspaper out of doors? But in much of Europe misunderstanding and persecution slowly gave way to respect and friendship, until in 1931, the Bishop of Oslo declared, at the laying of the foundation stone of the Norwegian Training College: 'Accept the thanks of the church which opposed you at the beginning because we did not know better.'

The Communists, however, continued to misunderstand and oppose.

In Russia the Army's official opening took place in a concert hall in Petrograd on an ominous date: 16 September 1917. Soon there were to be seven corps, two children's homes, two slum posts and an old people's home. But the October revolution was only weeks away, and from Finland, whence the Army had come, there came Lenin as well.

'On November 7th', wrote Commissioner Karl Larsson, 'I arrived in Petrograd unaware of the seriousness of the situation. In the afternoon we visited the quarters of one of our corps officers. Suddenly the street became ominously quiet. Looking out we saw that barricades had been erected at either end of the street and that soldiers lay behind them ready to shoot at each other. That night the Winter Palace was stormed and the resistance of the Women's Legion was drowned in blood. The fate of Russia and the work of The Salvation Army there was decided on that day for many years to come.'

The Army struggled on till 1922. 'When we tried to explain . . . how the Home had come to exist, we were asked why we still remained in Russia . . . the Soviet official . . . was very kind but clearly gave us to understand that the Soviet desired no prayers or any kind of religion in the education of children.'

The explorer Nansen put in a word for the Army, and Major Olsonti, the Finnish woman officer in charge, got as far as Kalinin's assistant. The latter was decisive: 'The methods of The Salvation Army differ in principle from the Soviet government . . . the Baptists and their like are Russian, but The Salvation Army is international. . . . Your Russians may organize themselves in some other way, but we cannot accept the international Salvation Army' (*Tio År i Ryssland*, by Karl Larsson, FA Press-Bokförlag, Stockholm).

What happened to 'your Russians' remains a mystery—but the Founder's song ('O boundless salvation, deep ocean of love') is still sung among Russian Baptists.

The antichrist from the left was followed by the antichrist from the right. Hitler took over Germany in 1933, and Europe, for centuries the heartland of the Christian faith, was fought over by two ideologies both of which were profoundly hostile to the gospel.

Hitler, like the Marxists, took a dim view of the Army. Field Marshal Göring might from time to time send gifts of game to the Army's homes, but this did little to offset the pressure of the Gestapo. From 1940–47 the Movement was led by Colonel Johan Büsing, who had to accept first of all a ban on military titles, and then, more seriously, an order to hand over all institutions to local authorities. This caused consternation in Hamburg, where the city fathers felt that the Army was welcome to carry on. Blind eyes were turned to the situation until mid-1943, when the problem was solved from above. In the great air raids on Hamburg, every Salvation Army property but one was destroyed.

Büsing did his best to provide pastoral care for the large numbers of foreign workers drafted into Germany. In Berlin, deported Dutchmen formed a Salvation Army band. At the Berlin Temple, meetings for worship were conducted in French. As late as the end of 1944, Büsing managed to arrange an international youth meeting in Berlin. This was too much for the Gestapo, who imposed a ban; but when the Berlin Temple was hit by incendiary bombs, a young Frenchman was first to put out the fire.

Nor did the Army lack souls with the spirit of Dietrich Bonhoeffer. 'Once, for a time', wrote Ilse Hille, 'I had to command the Hamburg Corps . . . I learned that one of the comrades, a Dutchman, had been sent to a concentration camp. I discovered that his sole crime had been the distribution of postcards inviting people to attend Salvation Army meetings. For many days I was busy going from one Gestapo office to the other; but not in vain. Within three weeks the comrade was released. When he gave his testimony, the German comrades in the audience wept.'

The Army in Germany survived, but its forces were cruelly depleted. The ancient struggle between Slav and Teuton brought the Poles to the banks of the Oder once again and Königsberg, where the Army's largest German corps had been, was renamed Kaliningrad.

In Italy too, the Army had a hard time: its leader, Brigadier Lombardo, was sentenced in 1940 to four years' imprisonment for 'developing defeatist attitudes under the cloak of religion while holding the position of Chief for Italy of the dissolved organization known as The Salvation Army, of English origin'.

But the dissolved organization would live to fight another day, and to face challenges—in the affluent West —more subtle and perhaps more insidious than the outright hostility of the Communist and the Fascist.

Over much of Europe the Army has now reached the third or fourth generation. A photo of the Army's history in Finland informs us: 'Tre generationer av Wahlstromska Salvationist-familjen'—and three generations of Salvationist Wahlstroms look solemnly at us. All bar the babies are dressed in uniform and one of them, a future International Secretary at International Headquarters, sits teddy-bear in hand on mother's knee.

That same history lists in Finland 59 corps, half of which were founded between 1889 and 1900. The rest, with three exceptions, came into being by 1920. Since then statistics indicate numerical standstill if not slow decline.

Here of course the Second World War made an evil contribution—for the loss of Karelia to the Soviet Union hit The Salvation Army as hard as Finland itself. But decline in religious belief—or at least in public religious observance—has been marked all over Western Europe: in Scandinavia as in Italy; in France as in Britain.

In some countries there are special difficulties. Few

English Salvationists are bothered, one way or the other, by proposals to disestablish the Church of England; but in Norway, whose Parliament appointed a commission in 1971 to consider relations between Church and State, the proposed disestablishment of the national Lutheran Church poses problems for Salvationists too. Many of them—uniquely in the Army world—have continued to regard themselves as members of the State Church and as Salvationists also. For them, as for other Norwegians, disestablishment poses an identity crisis. The Army's own commission was set up at the end of 1975 'with representatives for the old and young, officers and soldiers'. 'The process' . . . (of studying the Army's status as a denomination in Norway) 'must go on for a considerable time and must not be hurried. Our main aim' (writes the Territorial Commander) 'is to secure the Salvation Army's liberty and possibility of functioning in the future according to our call and tradition.'

But legal disestablishment of the Church of Norway is only part of that moral disestablishment that has over-taken Western Christianity as a whole. In questions of faith and morals Christians can no longer assume that their view—whatever it may be—will be accepted by society as a whole. 'It has been evident for a long time' (wrote Clifford Longley in *The Times* on 24 May 1976) 'that the generation educated since the war is a generation largely indifferent to, and agnostic about, religion. . . . The churches may find in the not too distant future that they have come to depend on a rump membership consisting of those families who, against the odds, manage to pass on religious beliefs in the home, together with whatever adult converts can be won from the agnostic community at large.'

Statistics from Norway—which has the largest Salvation Army in proportion to population of any country in the world—may be taken as fairly typical of the Movement in Europe as a whole.

In 1973 the Army in Norway had 11,847 soldiers and recruits. In 1975: 11,711. Average attendance at meetings decreased slightly, from 19,780 to 19,019. 'We have less outsiders coming to the Army,' writes the Territorial Commander, 'but our own people show signs of more serious concern: a main reason for the decrease is that we have 35 corps without officers.'

Static membership, of course, by no means implies that a Movement is folding up. On the contrary, it indicates that losses by death and resignation are being balanced by gains from new arrivals; though in some Western countries numerical decline may well be sharper than in Norway. 'Fewer outsiders—but our own people more serious' could be a common experience of the European churches today.

Clifford Longley again: 'All the churches, in their own interior life, are on paths divergent from the memories and expectations of the majority who opted out, or who were never in . . . a visible distance now separates the churches from the mainstream of national life. . . . Modern Christianity is now unknown and unexplored territory . . . an alien subculture. . . .'

Perhaps, however, the shock is less severe for the Salvationist than for members of the great national churches. He has always known of the visible distance that separates his own subculture from the mainstream. His uniform, his total abstinence, his busy week-night-and-all-day-Sunday programme of activities . . . have made him aware that he is not as other men are. And the process of renewal, for him, may be less jolting. He has no Latin mass to abandon; he does not have to exchange Cranmer's Prayer Book for the simplicity—or banality—of Series Three Communion. No particular translation of

the Bible is prescribed for his public worship, and so
there is no last ditch stand to be made for the Authorised
Version. In Britain, God is assailed by bad grammar
as 'thou' grudgingly gives ground to 'you' in public
prayer.

Shortage of vocations to officership remains a major
problem. The highest-ever intake of cadets to the William
Booth Memorial College in London took place during the
peak years of unemployment—since when better education has brought the young Salvationist opportunities
that his forefathers never knew. To the boy and girl
drawn towards the caring professions there are now other
avenues—teaching, medicine, the probation service, social
work—which are far better paid and do not involve the
privations of officership. But if quantity gives cause for
concern, quality is good. In the 1970s the Army has, for
example, been able to extend its work to Spain and
Portugal.

Enrique and Raquel Rey belong to Protestant families
in Corunna; it was as 'foreign workers' in Switzerland
that they met The Salvation Army. Enrique Rey, with
the zeal of an out-and-out convert, became Recruiting
Sergeant at Geneva Central: but his warmest desire was
to see 'El Ejército de Salvación' established in his native
Spain. When greater freedom of religion was promul-
gated in Spain the Reys were ready. Commissioned as
Captains in Zurich on Ascension Day 1971, they began
work in their native Corunna. On Christmas Eve it was
announced that the Army in Spain had won legal recognition.

In Portugal Agostinho Pereira had heard about the
Army from his father who had encountered it in Brazil.
But only when he read the life of William Booth, translated into Portuguese on the other side of the Atlantic,
did he find an address to write to. Thus it came about

that Major and Mrs Carl Eliasen, both Brazilian born;
arrived in Lisbon to begin the work of the Army. The first
cadet—Maria Lobão—went to study in Brazil with the
small group of Brazilian cadets.

The new Iberian Army is hardly likely to sweep forward
on a wave of religious awakening such as moved Protestant
and teutonic Europe in the 1880s: though there are,
in the traditionally Catholic countries, a large number
of dechristianized people who may well find the Army's
version of practical Christianity relevant and challenging;
certainly the poorer parts of Lisbon give the Army plenty
of scope—but will it be necessary, one might ask, to
export not only the Army's faith but its distinctive culture
—the English brass band, the navy blue uniform, the
timbrel brigade? Here is an ancient missionary dilemma—
new members of a small and largely unknown organization
can often define their identity only by adopting the culture
—heaven help us, even the hymns—of big brother across
the sea. Calls for native music, folk song and architecture
often come from the foreigner who can afford to be open
minded. To the man in the bush it is self-evident that
churches ought to have pointed windows and tall steeples;
it is often the missionary, who does not know what the
tomtoms are saying, who wants to introduce them into
matins.

Different methods but the same message? Nowhere is
the contrast between 'then' and 'now' more clearly seen
than in Switzerland, which gave the infant Salvation
Army a rough welcome indeed.

Geneva expelled an English evangelist, using note-
paper headed 'IHS' which meant—in Latin—Jesus
Saviour of Men. The canton of Vaud turned Captain
Charlotte Stirling, a young pioneer missionary sent out
from England, into a second prisoner of Chillon. Josephine
Butler, English champion of women's rights, travelled to

Switzerland and wrote a 300-page book pointing out the sad failings of the allegedly democratic Swiss. But nowhere was opposition to the Army more bitter than in Neuchâtel, once home of the great Protestant Reformer Farel. Neuchâtel even dared to imprison the eldest daughter of William Booth. In Neuchâtel 9,444 citizens signed a petition claiming that The Salvation Army was an attempted comeback by the Jesuits In Neuchâtel the Council of State denounced the Army's Swiss friends— the 'false Christianity of the protectors of Booth's Army', and declared—after Catherine Booth the younger had been driven over the frontier—'The Salvation Army no longer exists in the canton of Neuchâtel'.

Those were the days? 'Out of this', reported the fiery Railton in 1885, 'we have already got twenty-three men and women officers', plus 'a saved nihilist, sent by his comrades to blow up the government palace in Bern'. At the time of his conversion he had hidden in his house three bombs of dynamite, several revolvers and a dagger. These he returned, not to the police but to his fellow nihilists. They pointed a revolver at him threatening to shoot him; he calmly answered: 'Do it. I am ready to meet my God.'

Neuchâtel held out in opposition to the Army even after the Federal Courts had ruled in its favour: even when the President of the Confederation, Louis Ruchonnet, had pointed out that public attacks on the Army bore an uncanny resemblance to first-century criticisms of Jesus Christ, Neuchâtel still held out for a full year. Only in 1882 was the Army's hall reopened. 'The Salvation Army flag salutes the national flag', declared the Swiss *War Cry*. The Salvationists triumphed with a Hallelujah Tea, and Major Fornachon, perhaps to presage invasions of German-speaking cantons, and perhaps to demonstrate that the Army was not a conspiracy from 'foggy England'—sang a song in the dialect of Appenzell.

But these are tales of battles long ago. Nowadays the State of Neuchâtel owns the estate of Le Devens where the Army maintains a land colony. Mixed farming is the policy, with wheat, oats, barley, cattle and pigs; plus one working horse and two *en pension*. 'Farming', says the 1975 report, 'is the present framework for the picture of our home.' In the home there reside, upon average, between twenty and thirty men, more Protestant than Catholic, more single than married, more middle-aged than young: the unblest tie that binds them is alcoholism.

'Acceptance' (Accueil) writes Captain Walter Vogt, 'is the key word for effective social work . . . acceptance even for the person who cannot adapt to our society. Unlike drugs, alcohol is socially acceptable . . . it is rarely missing on social occasions . . . yet if someone becomes a victim of alcohol, that very same society rejects him. . . . What intolerance! Yet it can be well understood that these "fringe" people are met with reserve, or even with resistance. . . . To accept someone is to meet him where he is, as he is, with all his problems.'

Captain Vogt has three 'A's to sum up his policy. After 'Acceptance' comes 'Application'. Occupational therapy is more than leisure activity or simple self-expression work: it is work which demands commitment. Lastly comes 'Affection'—'the best means of re-establishing a personal relationship . . . when human relationships develop satisfactorily the need to drink decreases rapidly, and so does the desire to escape from one's problems in alcohol'.

Life at le Devens is not all work for the residents: in addition to producing 88,200 litres of milk and 25,179 kilograms of wheat, they found time, in 1975, to visit the Suchard chocolate factory, to watch the film *Papillon*, to

go on a trip by boat, to listen to a sermon by Pastor Rollier, to entertain the La Mouette Theatre Group, to hear Croydon Citadel Songsters from London, to see Brigadier Grossenbacher's slides on Israel. . . .

They also found time to produce a magazine—the *Courier du Devens*—which lets us know what the inmates —sorry—residents—think about the place:

'Coming back to the land of my childhood, and following the paths along which I ran with my mother. I'm as happy with my friends here as at home.'

'The piggery produces a good selection of magnificent piglets . . . I'm happy to help M. Thoerig in running it. . . .'

'My health worries me a little. Otherwise I feel happy though I would prefer to live at home. . . .'

Thus the changing world of Western Europe has obliged the Army to update its social services as well as its evangelism. The State now provides welfare for its people and social work has become a profession complete with certificates, hierarchy and pecking order. Successors to Mrs Cotterell, who took fallen girls into her Whitechapel home in 1884, now need diplomas if they are to qualify for grant in aid. Ancient warehouses, taken over as hostels for the homeless in Victorian times, can become millstones round the neck of a reforming Captain. Of course it is undesirable for 80 men to sleep in one huge dormitory, but if you improve things by dividing the space into forty private cubicles you will put forty men out onto the streets of a London from which hostel accommodation is rapidly disappearing.

In the Netherlands the Army has done as well as any, and better than most, in keeping up with the times.

'In the hard winter of 1890/91', writes Lieutenant-Colonel A. A. Van Dalen, 'The Salvation Army opened its heated meeting-rooms on the Rapenburg in Amsterdam and in the Zweestraat in The Hague from ten at night until seven in the morning. This was the beginning of the Salvation Army's help to the homeless in the Netherlands. . . .

'At first we used the English word "shelter"—then the Dutch word "toevlucht": after work opportunities were added it became an "industrial institution", and since about 1950 we have used the term "social centre". The change of name symbolizes, as it were, the new vision of the problem of the homeless in our society.'

And the Dutch homeless, it seems are not all that different from their colleagues world-wide, displaying 'disturbances of personality, and resentments against others, which are projected onto society, to wives, employers, etc.'.

Does this change of language mean that the psychiatrists are taking over, and that old ideas of sin and salvation are giving way to new concepts of disturbance and adjustment? 'A psychiatrist is attached to our centre', writes Major J. P. Van Nee, 'his role is advisory. If treatment is thought necessary then a consultant psychiatrist is brought in, via the family doctor. The Director has regular discussions with the social workers of the centre, whereby the advice of the psychiatrist can be discussed.' But a 'plus' for the Army, according to Major Van Nee, is 'the fact that we base our work on a spiritual foundation'. Help to those in need is combined with social rehabilitation, plus 'our own principle . . . that we always try to present a spiritual dimension, whereby people can come into relationship with God. It is my experience that the people with whom we achieve this provide us with the best results'.

In other words we still do our best to get them converted.

Upgrading has taken place in prison after-care work, to which the Dutch Salvation Army makes a major contribution: 'After the war the number of professionals began to increase. Training in a Social Academy became essential.

'At present The Salvation Army possesses, in addition to the Central Office of Prison Rehabilitation in Amsterdam, 17 local offices with departmental heads, 30 social workers . . . and several hundred voluntary workers who are ready to stand by their fellow-men in need.'

But what is the specifically Army contribution to this kind of work? Once again J. Th. Hertjes emphasises the Movement's religious motivation. 'The Salvation Army's Founder insisted that a human being is a unity in which social and spiritual are not to be separated . . . "there is a divine spark in everybody . . .", he said, and so The Salvation Army has always felt impelled to offer help to those who might be reckoned hopeless from a purely human point of view.'

European man, secularized, affluent, often indifferent to the faith for which his forefathers lived, killed and died, generally respects the Army's good intentions but ignores the religious message. Nevertheless, the religious message, the Christian insight, remains for the Salvationist, the heart of the matter.

In America

What was more natural than that the first Salvationists should turn their thoughts towards North America? Two-way traffic across the Atlantic had existed since the days of the Pilgrim Fathers; and as we noted in chapter 4, several 'typically Army' customs may well have originated in the camp meetings on the American frontier. A prototype for the Army's first Commissioner, George Scott Railton, could be the American revivalist Lorenzo Dow, who reached England in 1805. 'Those who heard him felt a strange spell, as though they listened to a voice from another world. His face was pale and marked by smallpox; his eyes were curiously bright and piercing; he had dark hair that hung to his waist.' Dow helped to found a Quaker Methodist church at Stockton Heath in Cheshire, and 'his preaching shaped the conduct of the men who were to form the Primitive Methodist Church' (*The Quaker Methodists*, by Arthur R. Mountfield).

An American with a clear and direct influence on the infant Salvation Army was the revivalist, Charles G. Finney (1792–1875). He was the Calvinist who saw the light and accepted the great truth that Christ died for all men

AND WHO, CONSEQUENTLY, GOT
WHOLE POPULATIONS
TO REPENT AND BE SAVED

This was but the final phrase of the title page of a pamphlet of 1882 in which Finney was billed as 'The

Presbyterian Salvationist'. He did not believe that revivals of religion came in the Lord's good time—on the contrary, you had to go out and work for them. He also upheld the Wesleyan teaching about Entire Sanctification, and while staunchly maintaining that everybody could be saved, he also rebutted the contrary error—that everybody would be saved in the end anyway. The list of his revivals was long indeed—at Evans Mills, Gouverneur, DeKalb, Western, Rome (in America, not Italy), Utica . . . and finally in Boston. His lectures on Revival found favour in the sight of Catherine Booth, and were republished by the Army.

Thus it came to pass that in 1880 Salvationists set out for the United States in the same spirit in which men like Lorenzo Dow had left it. Eliza Shirley and her mother Annie, members of the Christian Mission, had emigrated to the United States and had started Salvation Army work in a chair factory in Philadelphia. When George Scott Railton arrived with a party of seven British girls they decided to attack the devil in New York, 'In Harry Hill's Variety Theatre on Sunday 14 March 1880, after which the Panorama of Uncle Tom's Cabin, Admission 25c'. The first notable convert was Ashbarrel Jimmie, a drunk with so many convictions that the judge tried sentencing him to attend The Salvation Army. Jimmy's regeneration created such a stir that it led to the establishment of the Army's first corps in New York.

Similar events took place in Canada.

Once again, migrants began the Army's work. When Joe Ludgate met Jack Addie at a gospel meeting he recognized a kindred spirit because Jack Addie sang a Salvation Army song. They started in London, Ontario, in 1882, wearing English policemen's helmets inscribed, 'Prepare to meet thy God'. By 1884 Canada was a Salvation Army territory, with a Commissioner to lead it

and a Skeleton Army to attack it. Opposition in Catholic
and French-speaking Montreal was less than some
expected. The magistrate who set the accused Salvationists
free remarked: 'They look for sinners; in that they
resemble the Good Shepherd'—and in 1886 the foundation stone of Territorial Headquarters in Toronto was
laid by William Booth's third son, Marshal Ballington
Booth.

But Ballington was not destined to lay many more
foundation stones. Transatlantic strains were already
threatening to break the Army in half. Without incor-
poration the Army could hardly function under United
States law, but William Booth wanted to remain sole
trustee, just as he was in England. Could 'property be
kept in the name of Major Moore' (the United States
Commander) 'but mortgaged to General Booth?' Apparently not, for in 1884 Moore seceded; but his breakaway
movement came to nothing, and the infant Salvation Army
survived. By 1895, however, the sad story was ready to
repeat itself, and the plot had thickened.

'The system of governing the work in this country from
a foreign centre by laws made by those unaware of the
needs and conditions of the country is neither wise nor
practical.' This heart cry came from Ballington Booth
himself, now in command in the United States: American
nationalism and democratic spirit were reluctant to accept
one-man rule by William Booth from London: Ballington
Booth, with his wife Maud, felt driven to secede and set
up the Volunteers of America. The day was saved—from
the official Army point of view—by William Booth's
daughter, the dramatic Evangeline Booth. When she was
hissed as a 'minion of British despotism' she wrapped
herself in the Stars and Stripes and cried, in true Barbara
Freitchie style, 'Hiss that if you dare!' More mass
desertions were averted—and two years later the Army

in the United States was incorporated—as Moore and Ballington had suggested in the first place.*

One further irony remained. In 1904 Evangeline Booth herself became National Commander of The Salvation Army in the United States. Her powerful, histrionic personality made her a national figure. Her lectures—in essence one-woman dramas with props ranging from a lighted cross to a live sheep—could fill the Metropolitan Opera House. Her sponsorship of 'doughnut girls' to care for the welfare of American boys on the Western front did more than anything else to win for the Army that public sympathy that it has never lost. 'It was no secret', writes Sally Chesham in *Born to Battle*, 'that she gathered around her leading lights of society's important professional and business people.' Princeton University invited her to speak on The World's Greatest Romance.

By the 1920s Evangeline Booth was pleading with her brother Bramwell—then General—to make the Army's highest office elective. Bramwell attempted, in 1922, to divide the United States National Command into three territories directly responsible to him at International Headquarters: he ordered his sister to move. But now the leading lights came to Eva's aid. An ex-governor of Ohio—among others—stated publicly that 'it would be as disastrous to the people of this country as to The Salvation Army if Evangeline Booth were moved'. Bramwell backed down—for him it was the beginning of the end that came with his deposition in 1929. The 'minion of British despotism' had turned out to be the champion of American democracy.

In the end The Salvation Army in the United States acquired a unique constitution. It is divided into four

* The Volunteers of America reported 'more than 30,000 members . . . in 1964' (Frank S. Mead, *Handbook of Denominations in the United States*).

territories—Western, Southern, Central and Eastern, with Headquarters in Rancho Palos Verdes, Atlanta, Chicago and New York. But unlike India or Australia—large nations which likewise form more than one Salvation Army territory—the United States possesses a National Commander in New York: Puerto Rico and the Virgin Islands also come under his overall command. He is therefore, a kind of 'mini-general'—if the word 'mini' can be applied to anything connected with the activist, and—to the outsider—the affluent United States.

The Commissioners appear to practise what Roman Catholics call 'collegiality'. Their conference looks rather like a House of Bishops. They—and not the National Commander on his own—authorize the *Manual of Salvationism* which defines the faith once delivered to the saints as understood in the United States. They—the Commissioners' Conference—issue statements on race and other social questions. Nothing quite like it exists anywhere else in The Salvation Army world.

A curiosity of Church history: the absconding Major Moore managed to patent The Salvation Army crest, topped with the crown of life. This left the mainstream Army with no alternative but to adopt a similar crest, differenced by the presence of the American eagle. Now (1976) the American Salvation Army has gone over to the International crest, crowned with a crown.

Constitutional crises apart, the North American Salvation Army has had a history not dissimilar to that of the Movement in other Western countries. A period of heroic pioneering brings much ridicule and persecution. As the Army's work develops, attacks are made on its good faith. Thus, for example, Edwin D. Solenberger, general manager of the Associated Charities of Minneapolis, alleged the Army's 'so-called charitable work' was intended largely to make money. Since he made the claim at the National

Conference of Charities in 1906, some at least took him seriously. In 1909 the Board of Overseers for the Poor banned the Army from collecting in the streets of Boston: it was, they said, 'degrading and demoralizing to the public'. But the local press took the Army's side, and the 'Battle of Boston' ended in heavy defeat for the overseers. On Thanksgiving Day the Army fed five thousand.

The First World War did more than anything else to change public attitudes. Thousands of servicemen who knew little good—or little of anything—about the Movement were impressed by young women who were living exponents of practical Christianity. A poet wrote—in a servicemen's paper on the Western Front:

> Tin hat for a halo—
> Ah, she wears it well,
> Making pies for homesick lads
> Sure is 'beating hell'.
> In a religion blasted
> By fire and flame and sword
> This Salvation Army lass
> Battles for the Lord.

Some contemporary Salvationists, and not only in America, are irritated by stories of the Army's good deeds done during two world wars; would not the old hoary myths be better forgotten? But few myths proliferate without a strong root in historical fact. To wear a tin hat for a halo—how better could you manifest the presence of an incarnate God?

Nearly a century after the arrival of Railton and the 'splendid seven' the Army in the United States has over 5,000 full-time officers. Eighty-one of them serve abroad, in countries ranging from Australia to Zambia. Thus the Army in the United States is not quite half as old as the

Republic itself, for the Bicentennial of which the National Commander, Commissioner William Chamberlain made three claims on the Movement's behalf:

'Firstly . . . it has cared for the unfortunate of American society. . . . In any social system whether of free enterprise or otherwise . . . there are bound to be those who . . . fall by the wayside. . . .

'Second, The Salvation Army has been able to support national aims . . . which have furthered the cause of national unity, moral strength and the pursuit of happiness. To the Salvationist, there are no racial barriers. Black is beautiful whether in or out of Salvation Army uniform, but especially if they want to join our ranks.

'Thirdly, we have been able . . . to create the spirit of hope by our message of the redeeming work of Christ. . . . However technically qualified are Salvationist social workers, they will not attempt what they consider an impossible task except in the power of and spirit of Jesus Christ.

'The American way of life has laid her hand upon the Movement so that, though part of an international body of salvation soldiers, its expression has been marked by American enterprise, efficiency and freedom.'

One symptom of American freedom is the willingness to publish meaningful statistics. At the Bicentennial celebrations there were 80,016 salvation soldiers in the USA plus a further 36,647 adults in community membership. The Army, therefore, has not become a mass movement; nor has it become predominantly black. But the list of its good deeds is out of all proportion to its numerical strength. Indeed, massive social services and disaster relief operations have given it—in America perhaps more than elsewhere—the image of a welfare rather than a religious body.

But whatever the image may be, the reality is religious:

the heart of the matter, as in all evangelical Christianity, is the soul's personal encounter with God in Christ: 'God, why are you looking at me?', writes Sue Hendron of Seattle: 'God, stop looking at me like that. You make me squirm. . . . Why do you bother me so much, God?'

Sue's prayer is called 'Squirming on a cold metal chair, at camp.' The great poets of the inwardness of religion, from St John of the Cross to Gerard Manley Hopkins, would have recognized her youthful dilemma as their own. For all activist and outward-looking Christianity depends, for its strength, on an infinity of personal decisions, on the personal walk of a teenager with his conscience, on the long loyalties of uncounted years. No difference of motive need separate Eliza Shirley in the chair factory in Philadelphia from the college-trained Salvationist of the 1970s.

Not that the Army has not changed. 'When I started half a century ago', writes former National Commander Commissioner, Edward Carey, 'the professional was suspect in our ranks. There was a general feeling in the organization that education and dedication proceeded in inverse ratio. In turn the professional took a jaundiced look at what he called "consecrated ignorance". Over the years we have moved to a mutual appreciation . . . Salvation Army officers in increasing numbers have qualified themselves for service in specialized fields.' 'Nevertheless', continues Commissioner Carey, 'a spiritual rebirth . . . is still at the very heart of the Salvation Army programme.'

As an example of the Army's grappling with a new problem we may take an unfortunate by-product of women's lib: the growth in female alcoholism. 'It's a sign of the times', writes Mary Stanyon of the *San Francisco Sunday Examiner and Chronicle*, 'that as drinking problems among so-called "respectable" families increase . . . contemporary mores have greatly decreased the need for pregnancy shelters.'

So the unmarried mother gives place to the alcoholic matron as problem number one. 'We sincerely believe', says Major George Duplain, 'that we now have a programme that will reach the middle-class, closet-drinking woman, and provide a dignified private chance to "get herself together". Already a judge in a northern California city has given a rich matron the choice; either she gets six months in jail for repeated drunken driving offences or she enters our programme.'

And Major Duplain's programme operates with that enterprise and efficiency which the National Commander feels is typically American. Detoxification—if things are that bad—takes place at the Army's rehabilitation centre. Then there will be thirty days' assessment with medical check-up and psychological counselling. Next the woman goes to Pinehurst Lodge, a former children's home, for up to a year. She will have nothing to pay, for the project finances itself through the clients' 'work therapy'. Many will go to the Army's social centre in San Francisco 'to assist in the huge workrooms where donated clothing is sorted, repaired and made ready for sale in the thrift shops'.

Major Duplain sees nothing wrong in combining business with redemption: 'Isn't it wonderful', he asks, 'to think that what a family gives our pickup trucks might be the means of getting a neighbour back into society, leading a normal, healthy life?'

But if 'go and never darken these doors again' rarely rings in the ears of a girl who has got herself pregnant, there are still plenty of young people who get into trouble and run away from home. In Atlanta, Georgia, the Girls' Lodge provides a port of call—welcome and unexpected— for many a runaway. Captain Judy Moore runs the place with humour, human interest and supernatural grace:

Here Starsky and Hutch, the TV detectives, could learn a thing or two.

'The Girls' Lodge', she says, 'is a place which says to any young girls stranded in Atlanta. "You don't have to sell your body for food to eat and a place to stay. . . . It's a place which says to the eleven-year-old runaway, "you're not alone: we can work it out together. . . . It's a place which tries to share a God-like love with all who walk through its doors, a love which says 'I love you' regardless of how you look or the language you use . . . a place to learn that everyone hasn't given up on you. . . ." '

That, of course, is the gospel as it has been lived and practised however imperfectly, ever since Jesus of Nazareth came into Galilee proclaiming the good news of God. There are, of course, theological and cultural variations, and the Army in the United States, notably in the South, is markedly more 'conservative' than in other parts of the world.

Nevertheless an open split between 101 Queen Victoria Street, London and West 14th Street, New York, is highly unlikely. It would be in nobody's interest. The decline of British political power has left the General—currently (1975) a Canadian, and previously Swedish—if not in a neutral corner, at least in a seat independent of the superpowers. Grumbling about International Headquarters is more likely to come nowadays from the hardpressed Britons, who may feel that too large a slice of their money and man-power goes into supporting it, and that their own territories are governed by a complicated system.

In Latin America the Army's story has been different: there it has encountered problems such as it faced in Catholic Europe. In spite of zeal and devotion no less earnest than that displayed north of the Rio Grande, the Army has remained thin on the ground. Nor has it shared in the rapid expansion that has made Pentecostalism one of the fastest-growing religious movements in the world. In 1976 it counts 62 centres of work in Brazil, 124 in Argentina, Paraguay and Uruguay, and 85 in Chile, Bolivia and Peru. These statistics, of course, hide an infinite variety of human response. In Bolivia 'hundreds of converts' are reported, with twelve cadets in training in La Paz. In Chile 'underprivileged children are one of the main concerns of the Army's social outreach' and the public maintains its support, as in the days of Allende, so in the time of President Pinochet.

A prototype Latin American Salvationist might be Eduardo Palaci. Born to nominally Catholic parents in a Peru that was still suffering from defeat by Chile, he met, at the age of eight, three Englishmen who were among the first evangelical missionaries to his native land. Ridicule and opposition caused the little Sunday school, with its Bible studies and magic lantern shows, to dwindle away. At last the remaining missionary, Henry Backhouse, died a disappointed man, but not before young Eduardo had promised him to preach the word throughout South America. For the child had undergone a conversion experience as indubitable at that of Augustine and Luther —and for him too it came through a great affirmation in Paul's letters: 'There is therefore now no condemnation to them which are in Christ Jesus.'

Somebody gave Eduardo a copy of Samuel Smiles' *Self Help*—a work which moved him as profoundly as it did his Japanese contemporary, Gunpei Yamamuro. With an unsuitable English grammar Palaci got through *Self Help* five times in three years. He then became a salesman for the Bible Society and wandered far and wide in Latin America until he met The Salvation Army in Panama in 1905. There he offered to translate for two women who were having a hard time with bad Spanish at an open-air meeting for workers on the new canal. By 1907 the wanderer had reached Kingston, Jamaica, for Salvation Army officer training: his studies were cut short by the great earthquake of 14 January. Six hundred people died, and the practical gallantry of the Salvationists helped to make up Eduardo's mind: 'When I saw the self-denial and sacrifice of these officers, so similar to that of the first Christians . . . I felt absolutely certain that this was the mission that I should fulfil.'

And fulfil it, he did, for over forty years. 'My country', he wrote on returning to his native Peru, 'is the whole of the Spanish American continent, but the soil to which I belong is the portion of the continent where God granted me the grace to be born.'

When Palaci travelled to the United States he was greatly impressed by North American Salvationism—'its material greatness . . . colossal buildings and social operations'. But the religion of the gringos was worth watching too. 'In the centre of Satan's kingdom . . . in Chicago', wrote Palaci, 'where the disastrous effects of alcoholism can be clearly seen, every night from 250 to 300 men gather . . . and many of them are rescued by the officers working there.'

Time changes, and Satan has many new devices to test the patience of the saints. Palaci never lived to see another evil that would establish an unholy bond between Latin and Anglo-Saxon America: traffic in drugs. In the 1970s numerous young Canadians and Americans would get stiff prison sentences for attempting to smuggle drugs into the United States from Mexico. And Mexican jails, if not just as you imagined them from the old Western movie, are a rude awakening for the college youngster who tried to get through customs for a bet, with cocaine strapped to his legs. The Mexicans cannot even speak English. . . .

But at least the women from The Salvation Army can.

Mrs Major Ferraez and Mrs Captain Lopez visit the imprisoned drug smugglers regularly, providing woollens for innocents who did not even know that Mexico City would be cold at 8,500 feet. And for Christmas dinner, in honour of the Word made flesh, the imprisoned North Americans each got a box dinner of Kentucky fried chicken.

Colonel Saunders' recipe might not be too well received in Cuba, where the Army is making a unique effort to survive above ground in a Marxist state. Here some modifications are called for: Divisional Commander Major Jesus Santos is referred to—at least on envelopes—as President—and Mr. Jesus Santos. For ten years no Territorial Commander from the Carribean and Central American Territory was able to visit. But in 1974 the Army's man in Havana was able to commission 13 new officers in the Anglican cathedral. It appeared that Salvation Army religion might not be the opium of the people after all: which was good news for a Territorial Commander whose far-flung parish reached from the Bahamas to Surinam, and required the use of six languages and even more currencies. One of those countries is Haiti: once a French slave-colony, then the arena of fearful racial war: then the first free black republic—and later the scene of long disappointment as political and economic standards failed to rise. In Haiti—if French may count as 'Latin'—are perceptible a number of the cross-currents that have carried The Salvation Army through the Americas.

For example, Henry Rostett emigrated from Sweden to the United States as a boy. He worked on a farm, became a Salvationist, and retired as a Divisional Commander in 1954 without ever fulfilling his ambition to become an overseas missionary. In 1960 he took a tourist trip to Haiti.

Here the Army had then been at work for ten years, in a land where primary poverty summons the churches to their ancient tasks of opening primary schools, child health clinics and hostels for the handicapped, in addition to prayer and praise. Rostett made himself an unpaid missionary, preacher and public relations man for an Army that had produced, in Fond-des-Negres, a worshipping congregation, a school for 700 children, a feeding centre and a children's home. The Army's first leader had been Swiss, and other missionaries had included Australian and Norwegian girls who had to talk to each other in Creole. Rostett fulfilled his long-delayed vocation by manning the Christmas kettle in aid of Haiti on the streets of Miami, Florida.

Is this paternalism? Why should extreme child poverty exist in Fond-des-Negres and not in Miami? Are the efforts of the Salvationists providing misguided support for an ancient system of exploitation? Were the overseers of Boston right about the degrading implications of the Christmas kettle?

Such thoughts may occur to theologians, and social scientists. They do not seem to worry the Haitians very much for they welcome Rostett, whether he arrives on horseback or in a jeep; whether he is preaching a sermon or building a hall—for like his Master, he is skilled in carpentry.

In school, children can perceive, by the strange intuition of the young, which teachers are 'all right' and which are not. So too with Christian mission whether in Fond-des-Negres or in the Bowery, in America or in the world, genuine love is its own best argument.

In Africa

In darkest Africa The Salvation Army was to face problems far different from those presented by darkest England. As missions go, the Movement arrived fairly late on the African scene, reaching South Africa in 1883, Rhodesia in 1891; in the 1920s, Nigeria, Ghana, Kenya, and Zambia (then Northern Rhodesia). In the 1930s came advances to Uganda, Tanzania and Zaïre (then the Belgian Congo) and across the river to French Congo as well.

The indefatigable George Scott Railton had done a good deal of pioneering. In Zululand he deplored the difficulties caused by language: 'For want of . . . knowledge much of the splendid heroism of our pioneers was, no doubt, thrown away. I doubt if the people ever understood why these kind men, who could not speak to them, had come to live near them.' Railton was well aware of the difference between the Western and the traditional world. He reported: 'The dread of walking in the darkness in Zululand is not merely due to the fear of snakes, but to the fear of ghosts. The Zulu is apt to set down every sickness and mishap to the working of an evil spirit; and we have, perhaps, the greatest difficulty of all in getting the people freed entirely from the strange fears to which their ignorance has made them a prey. These are . . . secrets not easily got at in a public meeting.'

When Railton reached Zululand, the impis had been defeated and white power had been imposed. But the Army's leading prophet was not likely to fall for anything so vulgar as racial prejudice. In his opinion Zulu sinners differed little from British sinners, and the Zulu dandy closely resembled the English dandy, though the former carried several canes whereas the latter sported only one. Returning to the city, Railton observed the beginning of that urbanization which was to challenge the churches all over Africa. On top of slum housing there was the problem of race. 'Natives', reported Railton, 'are not allowed to live in the streets where European houses are, but are sent to what is called a "location". . . . It is amazing that the people on the locations are not swept away by plagues and diseases, so very unhealthy are their surroundings. . . . The worst overcrowding of Western cities is princely . . . as to the amount of air that each person has to breathe during the night, when contrasted with the location hovels . . . but far worse . . . is the moral degradation that has resulted from treating the natives as a sort of superior cattle.'

Railton saw no virtue in the mine compounds either: '. . . which are simply large squares or sheds, with scarcely any windows. . . . These sheds do not contain a scrap of furniture of any description . . . drunkenness seems to be almost as general as it used to be in an English colliery village.'

As Railton was writing, the Boer War was in progress. Public reactions disgusted him, and he added a post-script: 'Amidst all the tons of paper occupied with denunciations of British or Boers, how many square inches of paper have been used to plead the interests of the peoples of Africa? Will the great God and Father of all much longer allow the white races, calling themselves Christians, to go on ignoring the rights and the highest interests of all other peoples?'

Two world wars later, when the wind of change has blown across the African continent—where does The Salvation Army stand?

Working conditions have changed out of all recognition since Railton and Jim Osborne trekked over Zululand. 'Four hours upon one of these great waggons behind some sixteen or twenty oxen, and you are only ten miles on your way.' Western dress was a menace if you had to cross rivers, and cycling was unthinkable 'unless someone invents a bicycle that can stand rocks and holes without number'.

Nowadays car crashes take a heavier toll than snake bite, and the impracticable nature of Salvation Army uniform only appears when you visit a community far inside the bush where roads remain as in Railton's day.

The Army has shared in the numerical growth of the Church in Africa south of the Sahara. It has won converts chiefly from rural people whose faith has been traditional paganism. These people make demands quite different from the underprivileged of the industrial West; they ask of the Churches what elsewhere is provided by the State: above all education and medical care. These the Army has sought to supply, though it was, for long, ill-equipped both in personnel and in mental attitude.

Writing of Europe's conversion to the Christian faith, H. A. L. Fisher declared: 'In every generation there were religious enthusiasts touched by the moral beauty of the Christian virtues or exalted by the contemplation of the Divine nature . . . but . . . the Goths, the Franks, and the Saxons went over to Christianity, not as individuals directed by an inner light, but as people subject to mass suggestion and under the direction of political chiefs. . . . The great mass . . . experienced no change of heart on conversion. . . . Yet even in the rude society of medieval Europe human sacrifice was stamped out, polygamy forbidden, and slavery put down' (*A History of Europe*, p. 186).

It was rather like that in Africa. Even Moshesh, the

great and good king of the Basuto, never got round to baptism, and when the ever-hopeful Railton wrote of the 'Macedonian cry' that summoned the Army to Africa, he failed to mention that the cry was often made with mixed motives. 'I will bring many religions to my village', wrote one Nigerian youngster in the mid-1960s 'so as to have good hospitals, schools and clinics.' Why not?

A more judicious Salvation Army scout than Railton—who nearly died when he got to Accra—was Staff Captain Wilfred Twilley, who toured West Africa in 1917. In Lagos he found the Commissioner of Police 'politely antagonistic'; not so Bishop Tugwell of the Church Missionary Society; the latter recalled Railton's visit of a decade previously, promised 'full sympathy and blessing' and expressed concern because Railton had told him, on the basis of his South African experience, that the 'Army would receive as full members converts with several wives'. Twilley replied that Railton was 'a very tender and bighearted man', but that the Army would do nothing of the kind. Time would prove him wrong. Bishop Tugwell also made the tactful suggestion that the Army should move into unevangelized fields to the north, and keep off the claims staked by other missions. This advice the Army would ignore.

The Movement's line on polygamy was in fact perfectly defensible. Should a converted polygamist 'sack his wives'? If he is childless, should he not do the decent thing and take a second wife, like the ancient Hebrews? All Christian churches have faced this problem and have found it necessary to provide a half-way house for the polygamous Christian. Some allow him—and his numerous and often devout wives—to be baptized adherents but not communicants. The Army treats polygamists as it used to treat smokers, and admitted them to soldiership but not to local officership. But if 'Salvation Army soldier' equals 'communicant member' then clearly the Army allows polygamists one step further up the ladder than other churches do. This might not matter if you enter those unevangelized fields to the north. But in areas already occupied by other missions, whose ranks are already divided on the question, then you run the risk that polygamous dropouts—or victims of the system—will join you because your rules offer them a home. Thus it came to pass that in 1929 the Native Assistants—as the African Ministers were then called—petitioned against the Army's membership of the Christian Council of Nigeria on the grounds that it did not maintain proper standards with regard to Christian marriage.

Even stranger problems were confronted in Zaïre. When the Army arrived at Leopoldville in 1934 it presented—in the words of the evangelist Ernest Kimbembe —'A solemn gospel which penetrated deep into the hearts of the hearers'. But the pioneers, led by the Belgian Henri Becquet, were not to know that the lower Congo was a 'burned-over district': a land of people long ravaged by the slave trade, spiritually disinherited and longing for a redeemer. Here too was the home of the prophet Simon Kimbangu, an African Bunyan with no book but the Kikongo Bible, sentenced, like Christ his Master, to a political death for a religious message, and then reprieved to a living death in Elizabethville jail by the Belgian colonial regime. Was it not obvious—at least to the 'kimbanguist' underground—that The Salvation Army had come to prepare the way for the triumphant return of Simon himself? What else could be the meaning of the red 'S' on the missionary's collar? To shake hands with a European officer and suffer no mishap—would not this demonstrate one's innocence of witchcraft? And when the officer found out what was going on and refused to shake hands, could one not produce the same effect by standing

under the flag, or touching the red cord round the
Penitent-form? To destroy this delusion, iconoclastic
Colonels would cut away cords! In the end there emerged,
alongside the official Army, a syncretistic movement with
an odd variety of officials such as 'Pasteur', 'Capitaine'
and 'L'Etat'.

And when, in 1958, the Belgian administration at last
gave legal recognition to the Church of Jesus Christ
through Simon Kimbangu, a large number of crypto-
Kimbanguists left The Salvation Army and showed their
true colours. Such are the tragicomic misunderstandings
which can arise when a new faith is planted in the heart
of a strange and alien culture.

Anthropology was not a strong suit in the Army in
those days, though the Swedish researcher Efraim
Andersson is a little harsh when he says that 'all officers
were obliged to act in accordance with the directives
issued from the Army's headquarters in London, which
were quite unsuited to conditions in the field'.

Yet sociologists may dissect, and those who sit in the
seat of the scornful may laugh, but the elusive inwardness
of religion remains. Mbakanu Diakanwa, Territorial
Commander in Zaïre, was a mighty hunter in youth, until
in error he shot and nearly killed a man. Repentant, he
devoted his life to the gospel. Born in the heart of
Kimbanguist country he owns Simon as a true prophet—
though not, as the Kimbanguists claim, as the Comforter
promised in John 15.26. When the walkout took place,
after 1958, Diakanwa stuck to the Army for the simplest
and best of reasons: 'There I found the Lord.'

Much of the tension in the Congo arose because The
Salvation Army—like other late arrivals and breakaway
African Churches—did not accept the zoning arrange-
ments set up by the older missions. You ought to be a
Methodist, for example, if converted west of the Cross

River and a Presbyterian if you saw the light to the east.
One country where the Army got in first, and acquired a
zone of its own, was Rhodesia. The pioneers arrived not
long after Cecil Rhodes himself, and Jameson—he of the
Jameson raid—assigned to the Army 3,000 acres in the
Mazoe valley which became the site of Pearson farm. But
all was thrown into confusion during the Mashona
rebellion of 1896, when Captain Edward Cass was killed.
'When . . . venturesome horsemen picked their way
gingerly along the track the Salvationists and their friends
had journeyed, they found . . . the whitened bones, the
tunic and the brass "S"s of the brave Captain. . . .' It
was only after the Boer War that Fred Bradley and Joel
Matunjwa returned to develop the Army's work, and
with such success that by 1930 Rhodesia was constituted a
separate territory and by 1946 the Army possessed what
in other parts of Africa the people dearly desired to have—
a system of secondary schooling and teacher training.

In 1906 Lieutenant-Colonel Francis Pearce went in
for some doubtful generalisations not, alas, unknown
among missionaries in Africa. 'The Mashona', he wrote,
'is more a heathen than most of the tribes. His life is
largely made up of eating, drinking, fighting and *begging*.
"What will you pay me if I get converted?" is the extraordinary question often asked.' No doubt it seemed less
extraordinary to the doubly defeated Mashona, overrun
first by the Matabele and then by the Europeans. They
would not be able to take up arms for another sixty years,
by which time large numbers of them, having received
the treasure in spite of the earthen vessels, would be
Salvationists themselves and would face the dilemmas of
violence in Rhodesia from the other side of the fence.

The Army has put a large proportion of its missionary
effort into Central Africa. From Rhodesia it spread to
what is now Zambia, at first by natural 'seeding' among

the BaTonga, in whose territory arose the Chikankata Hospital and school. Here Colonel (Dr) William McAllister pioneered the training of nurses—no easy task in 1951, when only 7 girls in the entire country passed their 'Standard six'. Here too Brigadier (Dr) Sidney Gauntlett undertook responsibility for leprosy treatment throughout the southern provinces of Zambia, and was able to report that 'the average length of history had been reduced from 41·5 months in 1951 to 14 months in 1967. In other words, people were being cured of leprosy, and being cured much more quickly. '

Meanwhile, as the wind of change began to blow, the Army, like other churches had to trim its sails accordingly. Not all were able, like Sidney Gauntlett, to win the approbation of a future president. As Kenneth Kaunda wrote in *Zambia Shall be Free*: 'During the early part of 1958 I suffered a good deal from illness and the doctors could not seem to get to the bottom of it. I had one terrible journey from the eastern province when my lungs became full of dust. At that time, I was very grateful for all the help I received from the Salvation Army doctor at Chikankata, Dr S. C. Gauntlett. Not only did he do much in helping my recovery to good health, but on his busy rounds of the wards, he would stop at my bedside for long and interesting discussions. I am still glad to count him among my friends.'

Evidence of an agonizing reappraisal at Chikankata came when teacher Lieutenant David Wells suggested that the mission centre with its '500 students, 120 nurses and 300 plus in-patients' had led few to make a Christian commitment. According to figures given by the Evangelical Church of Christ, 'only 9 per cent of all Tonga are active Christians'. David Wells believes that this low score is due to lack of sympathy with traditional customs. 'Every time we have damaged or destroyed a traditional custom like girls' initiation or village beerdrink, without integrating a visible alternative, we have contributed to the destruction of the very fabric of society . . . what we teach is mainly external religion, so that being a Christian means "not drinking, not smoking, not having more than one wife, not observing the customs of the tribe, going to services, possessing a Bible, wearing a uniform, etc. . . ." '.

From externals to heart religion—it is the old dilemma of the Christian and the Puritan Christian above all. Can you baptize the beerdrink? Can you sanctify the girls' initiation ceremony? (We may note in passing that 9 per cent active Christians would be hailed with delight in many a downtown city church in the West!) Many a mission has set out declaring, hand on heart, that it had no intention of producing little replicas of suburbia in heathen lands afar—and in the end, apparently, has done just that! To separate the inward truth from the outward expression seems a puzzle too hard for every faith—for why else should London's devotees of Hari Krishna dress in garb more suitable for the banks of the Ganges than for Oxford Circus?

But it is easier to call for indigenous music and local theology than to sit down and produce it. Most Salvation Army song books in African languages consist almost entirely of translated English hymns. Words do not always make sense, and still less do tone patterns fit the tunes, but while this may upset the literary minded and disgust the educated young, it does not worry the devout for whom the traditional version is hallowed by years of loyalty and familiarity. For example, the Efik version of 'Are you washed in the Blood of the Lamb?' inquires whether your garments are spotless and white as 'sno'— a word without meaning. Research reveals that the comparable idiom among the snow-less Efik is 'as white as high heaven'—for perception of colour differs from people to people. But this genuinely local expression will not fit the tune, so the revision committee is left with the tame alternative: 'Are your garments spotless, are they clean . . .', which fits the metre after a fashion but does not stop the faithful—especially those who cannot read —from belting out, under roofs of thatch or corrugated zinc, the words 'white as sno' as they have done for generations.

Only African Christians, of course, can produce genuine African Christianity, and they are doing it all the time, although for example—most of the indigenous anthems they compose remain copied into school exercise books rather than printed in official hymnals. Sympathetic outsiders can help a great deal, but as Lieutenant-Colonel Gordon Swansbury, Chief Secretary in East Africa, declared: 'Having taken a group of cadets to visit a Bible College near Nairobi, I heard one of the residents ask, "What are you doing to Africanize Christian theology?" To which I replied rather bluntly, "Nothing; only you can do that." '

If you want to produce African theology you must of course have African theologians, and here the Army has been handicapped by the inadequacy of its education programme. The old insights of George Fox—that being bred at Oxford or Cambridge fits no man to be a minister of the gospel—is of little use when you try to provide a literate and thoughtful ministry for village churches. The Army has indeed sought to raise its educational requirements, but it has remained behind the teaching profession and indeed behind other denominations as well. The Army's training course may be as long as that given to catechists of other churches, but should the officer be publicly equated with a catechist then grave problems of status can arise. Officership is so poorly paid that there

are few chances of attracting the African professional
with his numerous relatives to support. Bengt Sundkler,
in *The Christian ministry in Africa* suggests a two-tier
ministry for the African Church, with higher paid and
more highly educated pastors to serve the more affluent
city congregations. That option is not open to the Army,
which has always given higher pay and recognition to
seniority and rank, not to educational qualifications.

Meanwhile the Army must still try to find qualified
leadership for both the rural and the city congregation . . .
but what will the pressures of secularization and urbanization do to the African Church? Will the industrialized
working classes be lost as they were in Europe? In Nigeria
the well-filled hall is more often found in the bush than
in the city, while an officer at the other end of the continent wrote of the disintegrating effects of the South
African system upon rural life: 'Every corps . . . is over-
whelmingly composed of women and girls . . . I have
rarely conducted revision of rolls, when a name has not
come up . . . old heads have been shaken, perhaps eyes
have filled with tears, and someone has said: "He went to
Johannesburg (or Durban, or Cape Town—as the case
may be) many months ago, and now we no longer know
of him." '

Meanwhile, though 'a heritage of animism and the fear
of the supernatural are potent forces in all Bantu life' the
educated young are aware of other challenges. Young
African Christians can agonize over Charles Darwin,
evolution, and the truth of Genesis, as painfully as young
Englishman did a century before. 'I had a book about
science', writes nineteen-year-old Deborah Ekanoye.
'This book became my companion. I argued on it frequently. I became engrossed in it. I even told my friends,
"There is no God. We were all animals before." I was
blaspheming many times unknowingly.' Deborah, born in

England to a Yoruba father and an English mother, has ended on the side of the angels. Her spiritual pilgrimage has taken her from the Roman Catholics to The Salvation Army via the Eternal Order of Cherubim and Seraphim and the Redeemed Christian Church. 'I assure you', she tells her fellow Nigerians, 'that Jesus is the greatest.'

Articulate girls are welcome voices in the Church in Africa. Schooling has generally been granted to boys first of all, and so the women, like women in much of the world, are unable to express their views in public either because they cannot write, or because they cannot speak the language of the educated. The West African *War Cry* that carries Deborah's views on science and religion has often featured questions as to why Salvationist women do not keep silence in church in accordance with the second letter to Timothy. The questions are, of course, sent in by men.

While the Army has stuck to its policy about the ministry of women, it has had a rule—in Africa—to accept only married couples for training. The single woman, pursuing a career, seems to traditional Africa a rare bird if not an odd one. Fears of moral mishaps, real or imaginary, led to long hesitations, but now the plunge has been taken and single officers, male and female, have been commissioned. The rule that an officer can marry only another trained officer still applies, with an odd cultural side effect: on one occasion traditional betrothal ceremonies were accompanied by an intelligence test!

One might suppose that the Army's simple ministry would enable its officers to keep closer to the people than are the desk and pulpit-bound intellectuals of the historic churches. But it is doubtful whether this has proved true on any wide scale. The Army is, after all, as much linked to the West as are, for example, the Methodists and the Presbyterians—perhaps more so, for senior appointments

are made by the General in London. That indigenous,
down-to-earth ministry so longed-for by William Booth
in his own day, has to a large extent been provided, in
Africa, by the numerous apostles, prophets, prophetesses
and seers of the independent churches that have sprung
up all over the continent.

Yet the universal message of Christianity has taken
root in Africa; and The Salvation Army's planting, if at
times starved of air and water by the more powerful
shoots growing near by, is none the less alive and growing.
Africa has travelled far in a few decades. The testimony of
Colonel Joshua Ngugi, now the Army's Territorial Commander in East Africa, illustrates how great the distance is:

'Once upon a time I was a small boy of the Kikuyu
tribe. . . . My father had no education whatever, but was
skilled in trading his tobacco for sheep and goats with the
Masai. When I was about eleven I was sent by my father
to the common grazing ground owned by the Kikuyu. . . .
All day I would wander around watching our flocks. One
day when my father visited me I asked to be allowed to
leave the flocks to a younger brother so that I might seek
other work. I secured a job at a wattle factory. . . . Among
the employees were some girls who were working during
the school holidays. They sang the hymns of their mission
school. "My Jesus I love Thee" caused me to shed tears,
although I hardly knew why.

'My mother helped me occasionally with money which I
felt I should give to the church. One day I was given a
sheep by my father, and went off happily to find a grazing
space for it. I was stunned to find on my return that my
father had slaughtered it for a sacrifice. He tried to insist
on my sharing the meat, but I refused and said that I
would pray to God for food. As I wandered disconsolately
in the bush a tiny dik-dik—the smallest of the African
antelopes—crossed my path, and though it was fleet of

foot I managed to catch it . . . My father's party believed that God had provided me with food.

'I finally left and found work as a garden boy to an English family at Nakuru. I became interested in The Salvation Army through reading the *Sauti ya Vita* (the *War Cry*). I became a Salvationist. . . .

'Reading my Bible one day I became especially interested in the book of Joshua . . . I chose the name Joshua for myself. There was no dedication service, no christening ceremony; only I acknowledged that I wanted to serve God and be used as was Joshua of old. . . .'

In Africa the Christian Church has known many false starts and false dawns. Now—in spite of its educational, financial and even ethical shortcomings—it has established deep roots in the moral awareness and spiritual perception of African people.

In Asia and Australasia

India was The Salvation Army's first overseas mission field. What was more natural than that soldiers of the King of kings should turn their attention towards the great Empire garrisoned by soldiers of the British Queen?

Potential missionaries were there already. Frederick de Latour Tucker, Assistant Commissioner and Magistrate, was so ardent a Christian that he used to take his clerk to the crossroads and preach to passers by. This practice was felt, by the authorities in Simla, to be incompatible with his political position. They told him to stop, and stop he did, but with a troubled mind. A Christmas issue of the London *War Cry* reached him, together with a receipt for a donation he made to Salvation Army funds. Stirred by William Booth's article on the prophet Nathan, Tucker went on leave to London, tied a red ribbon round his hat and told his friends he intended to join The Salvation Army. In 1882 he returned, leading a pioneer party of six, which was reduced to four by the time they got to Bombay. There they were welcomed by a large detachment of the police, for the authorities feared that the much publicized attack by the sensational *Muktifauj* might lead to a riot. Not for nothing had the Honourable East India Company struggled to keep all Christian missions out of its domain! Imperial India could do so no longer, but street processions were banned, and The Salvation Army flag was impounded as a likely affront to Muslims.

The net result was to get the Army off to a good start. Missionaries saw the Movement as a champion of evangelical freedom, and some Indians viewed it as a fellow-victim of the imperial establishment. The Hindu reformer, Keshab Chandra Sen, protested to the Viceroy. To Tucker he wrote: 'You have been most unkindly and unjustly persecuted because your love for God and Christ exceeds the limits of conventionalism.' 'Could The Salvation Army', asked the press, 'doff lavender-coloured breeches and Christy's patent helmets to put on the mendicant's garb? Could it dance, shout, and march with the ordinary proletarian human nature from the mill?'

Tucker was certainly determined to try. Missionaries should wear only native sandals, if they could not achieve perfection and go barefoot. Uniform should be of that saffron hue which typified the soul dedicated to God, with a red jacket to provide a Salvation Army touch. Western furniture should be replaced by Indian furniture, or better still, by none at all. Local food only should be eaten, and missionaries should follow the Hindu custom and beg from door to door. 'To tell an Indian', wrote Tucker, 'that The Salvation Army disgraces the religion of the ruling classes by adopting a native dress, begging for food and going barefoot is sheer nonsense. In the eyes of an Indian, religion means self-denial. To connect it with self-indulgence and then dress it in foreign garb is to him simply disgusting.'

Tucker was determined to practise what he preached. Indian names were to be adopted. The Territorial Commander became Fakir Singh.

Alas for the hopes of the heart and soul idealist! The threads that bind Christianity to Western culture are not so easily snapped. Tucker had his critics, who felt that there was madness in his methods. 'Delicate European ladies', wrote one of them, 'were subjected to degrading

conditions of life . . . some died from enteric, cholera and
other oriental diseases.' Pain of the pioneers, it seems, like
the blood of the martyrs, can prove to be the seed of the
Church. Among those who died was Tucker's wife who
had 'collected funds . . . barefoot and in native dress,
among ladies of the social circle in which she had previously moved'. So hot was the controversy over Tucker's
methods, that in 1886, following the Army's first International Congress, William Booth went to India to see for
himself. The result was a diplomatic compromise. Tucker
was officially upheld, but his methods were modified.
Missionaries ceased to beg for rice or live in huts. Medical
care became the order of the day, and if you provided for
the health of the Western missionary you would have to
do something, sooner or later, about the health of the
Indian too. Enteric, cholera and other oriental diseases
were no respecters of persons.

In the last quarter of the nineteenth century The
Salvation Army spread rapidly in India. True to its
mission, the Movement sought out the untouchables of
Hindu society, and many of the casteless people responded
to its message, as they did to that of other Christian
groups. In 1893 Harry Andrews opened a dispensary at
Nagercoil in South India. Cholera in Travancore—now
part of Kerala State—then called him to a wider field of
medical work. Hearing that a Dr. Percy Turner had given
up his practice to become a Salvation Army officer,
Andrews begged him to come over to India and help.
Succeeding, he persuaded Bramwell Booth to persuade
William Booth to appoint Captain Percy Turner as the
first qualified medical officer to the Catherine Booth
Hospital at Nagercoil. The old man took some persuading.
Might not the care of sick bodies divert attention from
the salvation of perishing souls? But at last he agreed.
The Army's medical work had begun—and at Nagercoil

they preserve a relic: the door of the bathroom where Andrews set up his first dispensary.

Andrews qualified as a doctor himself, and went on to begin the Army's medical work in Gujerat. In dying he won the Victoria Cross, for by a strange irony the man whose sympathies lay with the turbulent tribesmen of the north-west frontier was killed by them. 'When a Ford car was available to collect the wounded,' said the official citation, 'he showed the utmost disregard of danger. . . . Captain Andrews seemed to bear a charmed life, but just as he stepped into the last van he was killed.'

That was in 1919—the year of the Amritsar massacre, when General Dyer's troops fired on a crowd of demonstrators. Gandhi's movement of non-violent protest was making headway: untouchables, the Mahatma declared, were in future to be 'Harijan', children of God, and Hindus ought to love them just as much as the Christian missionaries did. The long retreat from Empire had begun.

Booth-Tucker (Fakir Singh had married into the Founder's family and double-barrelled his name) was puzzled. 'There looms upon India's horizon today a new and remarkable phenomenon in the form of Ghandi-ism' [sic!] 'which cannot be repressed or ignored, creating as it does an entirely novel situation.' It was clear to Booth-Tucker that British rule ought to continue. 'It is an honest government in a country saturated with bribery and perjury. . . . It is a peaceful government. The Pax Britannica has prevailed for the last seventy years in a country as full of rivalries and jealousies as Europe.'

The answer to the Mahatma was the creation of an effective government press, in the vernacular, to counter the propaganda of the pro-Gandhi press. Village headmen should be taken into confidence and shown that the non-co-operation policy might lead to a renewal of the ancient struggle between Hindu and Muslim, with chaos or bolshevism to follow. Ringleaders, meanwhile, could be deported or placed under restriction, and martial law employed to deal with riots.

Tucker was old and ill and perhaps out of his depth, but he was still Fakir Singh. He knew and said plainly that the Raj could not be maintained at bayonet point. If only those ringleaders could be winkled out! If only the people would buy pro-government newspapers! Tucker believed that money spent in putting the government's case would in the long run be recovered from a convinced and reconciled India. Similar arguments—one must admit in all fairness—are often heard today in support of military and authoritarian regimes throughout the Third World.

But for British India it was not to be. If Britain possessed the goodwill she lacked the power, and in the Second World War the Japanese conquest of much of South-East Asia would put paid to the pretensions of the British, French and Dutch. Would the end of Western political power mean the end of Western religion? Thomas Hobbes, the seventeenth-century philosopher, unkindly compared the Pope to the ghost of the Roman emperor, sitting crowned upon the grave thereof. Would The Salvation Army turn out to be the spectre of the British Empire, fading away along with the memories of Christy's patent helmets?

The answer is no. Christianity is a universal faith, not simply a by-product of Western colonialism. Acclimatized to the soil of the orient, it has put down deep roots which neither the partition of India nor the secession of Bangladesh have been able to destroy.

Yet the climate of opinion is far different nowadays. The Indian Salvation Army is a minority group in a minority religion. The days of mass conversions of untouchables are long over. Some aboriginal hill peoples who have made the faith their own have been drawn into conflict with the central government. In their villages the loudspeakers of the Indian Army play hymns in praise of the Lord Krishna, not the Lord Christ. One unfortunate Salvation Army Captain was arrested because he happened to have the same surname as another Captain, the leader of the insurgents across the Burmese border. Entry by overseas missionaries is now restricted and the quota of available visas must be carefully husbanded. 'We lost two', says a report, 'and now we have little chance of getting them back again.' In other words, no overseas personnel were available when replacements were needed, and so the precious visas were lost. In Burma no expatriate missionaries have been allowed to live for years.

Most challenging of all is the opposition of Eastern religion itself, coupled with national sentiment. 'Many of our Hindu friends', wrote the Indian Christian thinker, Dr P. D. Devanandan, 'have expressed severe criticism of our missionary work. One objection is that Christian evangelism in India is an anti-Indian activity. The other school . . . denounce the work of Christian evangelism on the score that it is contrary to . . . the Hindu belief that all religions lead to the same goal, and should therefore be viewed with mutual "tolerance". Such tolerance is fiercely intolerant of what is described as "proselytism"—the "giving up" of one religion in order to "go over into another . . ." ' (quoted in Stephen Neill, *The Unfinished Task*, p. 294).

'The Christian must not be surprised', writes Bishop Neill, 'if, between now and the end of this century, the work of Christian witness in India becomes more difficult than it has been for a century.'

All will depend, of course, on the faith and integrity of the Indian Christians themselves: and the Army in India is almost as old as it is in Britain. Generations have been brought up in loyalty to the yellow, red and blue flag, to the memory of the Booths, to the simply furnished hall and its Penitent-form. If the inadequacy of the Army's education programme has left it short of qualified leadership, its down-to-earth faith has produced plenty of committed Christians in town and village, among those who follow the plough as well as those who cling to the trams of Calcutta.

And in Calcutta there is plenty of scope for the Army's 'traditional'—as the public would see it—work of feeding the hungry. Here Major Dudley John Gardiner (ex-Indian Army major, that is) maintains a feeding programme for six thousand people a day. It is all in a day's work to visit a room full of coffins—for the coffin-maker has to store his wares inside, while sleeping outside himself—and discover an elderly Anglo-Indian woman living on a pension of 135 pice per day. New clothes, new bedding, and contact with a nephew in Australia—these are the nourishing ingredients of practical Christianity, according to Dudley John Gardiner's recipe.

Yet The Salvation Army in the sub-continent—seven territories from Pakistan to Sri Lanka—also maintains medical work requiring the highest surgical skills. The report of the MacRobert Hospital at Dhariwal in the Punjab, for example, lists numerous operations only some of which are comprehensible to the layman. 'Repair harelip—2' means, no doubt, an end to personal humiliation for somebody, as does 'Repair of club foot—2'. The uninitiated will be less certain about the good done by 'chalazion extraction—4' but from the context it clearly has something to do with Christ's command to restore sight to the blind.

Yet a question mark hangs over the historic mission hospitals of India. 'The bigger one becomes,' says the report from Dhariwal, 'the bigger the problems become also . . . the need to upgrade the hospital is acute. . . . One recurring problem is that of staff.' A sad footnote to the report tells us that it was prepared by the Chief Medical Officer, Captain (Dr) Walter Lucas, who died on 22 August 1973, prior to publication.

So Christian missions in general and The Salvation Army in particular face a major rethink about their medical work throughout the Third World. Those famous hospitals, says Commissioner Harry Williams, FRCS (Edin.), FICS, 'are now in most instances . . . a millstone round the neck of the Church.' Where some would give up hospitals altogether, or switch the Church's commitment entirely from curative to preventive medicine, Commissioner Williams recommends, from long experience in Asia, 'a reduction in the size of many famous hospitals, with training for nurses at a simpler level than that of the State Registered Nurse'. At the same time there is a continued need for rural clinics and small hospitals 'manned by missionary nurses and aides of various kinds'.

The crisis in missionary medicine only reflects the crisis in world medicine. As the art of healing grows ever more expensive, the sick suffer from the iron law: 'To him who has shall be given, and from him who has not shall be taken away even that which he has.' As British doctors leave to better themselves in North America, Asian doctors move into Britain to take their places—but who is left doctorless at the end of the line? Governments are as likely as churches to nourish expensive white elephants in the shape of prestige hospitals and medical schools. They rely, however, on compulsory taxation not on voluntary donations. So there seems no way of reversing the trend apart from applying the principles of Jesus and putting service before profit. In the outback of the Third World the mother-to-be still needs that rural clinic, not too many miles of dirt road away, and staffed by someone who is accessible, competent and kind . . . perhaps a Catholic sister, perhaps a Salvation Army Captain.

Moving from India to the Far East, the traveller who searches for The Salvation Army will find a group of people who, in the idiom beloved of the old Puritans, 'have the root of the matter in them'."

The Japanese Salvation Army underwent hard testing during the war. Were they not a fifth column for the Western powers? Zealots even managed to discover hints of treason in Yamamuro's *Common People's Gospel*—a national best-seller that had been presented to the Emperor. In 1940 the Territorial Commander was arrested for a while, and the Movement was renamed the 'Japan World-Saving Organization'. In 1941 it was merged, by government decree, with the United Church of Japan—a shotgun union of all the Protestant churches. Ordination and the sacraments were accepted by some, but for many Salvationists the unexpected merger was not something to praise the Lord about. One Major with limited English summed it up plainly: 'Last in—first out!'

Yet even then the Army did not disappear entirely, for its social services continued as 'The Japan Mercy Christian League' under Major (but Major no longer) Mitaro Akimoto. As the tide of war began to flow against Japan, the Mercy Christian League found plenty to do. The Army's hospital and sanatorium were bombed. Numbers of Salvationists were conscripted and many killed. Yet within a few days of the war's ending open-air worship was held in a suburb of Tokyo, and on 22 September 1946 the Kyo Sei Kun—The Salvation Army under its old name—reappeared officially once again.

Those days of anguish were recorded by Tamiko

Yamamuro—now a Lieutenant-Colonel, retired—in her poem *In Prison*:

WAR . . .
>   And the heavy hand
>   Of thought police
>   Upon our band,
>   Because we call ourselves an Army
>   And proclaim that Christ is king;
>   Our possessions seized
>   And papers searched;
>   Our soldiers persecuted;
>   Leaders thrown into jail . . .
> . . . I think of Saul the persecutor—
>   He who died a saint!
>   And so I fix my mind
>   Upon the power of God.
>   Then hope comes back,
>   Hope for our jailers
>   And for this poor land I love!

Songs from the Land of Dawn (interpretation by Lois J. Erickson).

A later generation finds The Salvation Army grappling with the problems of powerful, wealthy, capitalist Japan. Booth Memorial Hospital in Tokyo began in wooden buildings surrounded by open fields. It was intended to provide a refuge in which tuberculosis victims might spend the rest of their days. Nowadays the urban sprawl of Tokyo has crawled round it and only a few of the original Himalayan cedars remain. The last of the rickety wooden buildings was demolished in 1974, to be replaced by a 140-bed hospital wing. Tuberculosis patients can now look forward, not to an asylum, but to cure and rehabilitation. The constant figure in this history of change has been the Medical Superintendent, Dr Nagasaki, who has combined his medical work with the spiritual role of a Salvation Army officer for the last 22 years.

Across the sea, in Korea, Salvationists have had, perhaps, even greater tribulations in the name of Christ. From beginnings in 1908 the work has been hard hit first by the Second World War—when, as in Japan, attempts were made to impose Church union by government decree. Recovery was then overwhelmed by the disaster of the Korean war. The Youth Band in Seoul was marched northward and disappeared. At least one Salvationist was martyred by the communists. The Territorial Commander, Herbert Lord, was interned for three years with other Church leaders by the Yalu river. After the war came those developments which have made the Church in South Korea as resilient and impressive as any in the world.

Major Paul Rader, whose thesis *The Salvation Army in Korea after 1945* helped to earn him the degree of Doctor of Missiology, feels that International Headquarters were rather slow off the mark in re-establishing contact with Korean Salvationists after the two wars: 'The sluggish response of IHQ to their needs has not been lost on Korean officers and soldiers. . . . If they seem to value their association with fellow Christians in Korea more highly than their commitment to the international Salvation Army and its representatives, one does not have to look far for valid reasons.'

Korean Salvationists show their Church attachments in such matters as calling the Songster Brigade a 'choir' and paying a fee to the organist. 'Unlike the Japanese', wrote one Colonel Stevens in 1924, 'they are not anxious to get into uniform and let everyone know that they are soldiers of Christ.'

As Rader points out, the same could be said of numerous Salvationists outside Korea too! But what does 'salvation' mean to the Korean Christian? For one, wearing clean clothes, learning to read, and studying the word of God. For another, deliverance from idolatry. For yet another, an approach to God through prayer rather than by reliance upon 'mu dang'—the local system of divination. Another describes it as 'peace of heart and a more disciplined life'.

In 1971 there were 22,167 salvation soldiers in Korea, with a total 'Army community' of 68,314. One young man was asked, in Rader's questionnaire, to explain why he stuck to a rather divided, not very successful congregation. The reply illustrates that common conviction which confronts us throughout the Christian world and which is either the supreme reality or the supreme illusion. 'My father found Christ through Envoy Tak [the local pastor] who also helped him in his business . . . I feel this was the will of God: that he be led to the Army and that all our family receive salvation.' Once again faith and works go together. Would the young man have been so impressed if Envoy (in non-Army language 'lay preacher') Tak had not helped his father in business as well as things spiritual?

The same personal and practical commitment to Christ finds expression in a more 'Western' Salvation Army hundreds of miles to the south, in Australia and New Zealand. The first Salvation Army open-air meeting ever held in Australia was held under a gum tree in the Botanic Park, Adelaide, in 1880: the preacher, whose name was John Gore, was a ganger on the railway who had not waited for his Captain's commission to arrive from London before taking action. From these beginnings and from the invasion of New Zealand by two under-twenty-ones, Pollard and Wright, in 1882, has grown the Australasian Salvation Army, with two territories in Australia and one

which is a simplified version of the 'Swearing in of Soldiers' with which we began. They can remain 'junior soldiers' until they are deemed old enough to attend recruits' classes and, at the age of fourteen, consider signing the *Articles of War*. And if they decline to sign these, then, at the age of seventeen, they will have to be taken off the roll.

What percentage of the 8,000 young New Zealanders will become fully committed salvation soldiers? How many of them attain an adult personal faith in God? The issue will be decided by all kinds of factors psychological and spiritual, countless unremembered acts of love or indifference, innumerable moral decisions great and small. And the New Zealand teachers are reminded, in their handbook, that abstract theology is only the servant of inward faith: 'Nothing is more vital in creating a helpful atmosphere than the worker's personal relationship with Jesus Christ. . . . When you are with your young people Christ should be there too. . . .'

In the end, Salvationism turns out to be simple Christianity. Let four voices, in our epilogue, speak for themselves.

Postscript: Four Voices

. . . And now, comrades and friends, I must say good-bye. I am going into dry-dock for repairs, but the Army will not be allowed to suffer, either financially or spiritually, or in any other way by my absence; and in the long future I think it will be seen—I shall not be here to see, but you will—that the Army will answer every doubt and banish every fear and strangle every slander, and by its marvellous success show to the world that it is the work of God and that the General has been His servant. . . . While women weep, as they do now, I'll fight; while little children go hungry, as they do now, I'll fight; while men go to prison, in and out, in and out, as they do now, I'll fight; while there is a drunkard left, while there is a poor lost girl upon the streets, while there remains one dark soul without the light of God, I'll fight—I'll fight to the very end! (Extract from William Booth's last public address.)

Repose

O love, unfathomable, deep,
Thou who dost waver not, nor sleep,
Encompass me, and I'll not fall,
E'en though I hasten at Thy call:
'Come, O my own, into the night!
Leave the glad fields of joy and light,
Come from the hills and glistening meres,
Into the vale of pain and tears.'

O strong and faithful, earnest Love,
Thy stillness points to stars above,
And 'mid abysmal dark there shines
Treasure once hid in secret mines;
By hill or vale I have no care,
No fear assails—for Thou art there.

Catherine Baird, *Reflections*

As for the nature of our society, as long as there are broken homes and chronic alcoholics, compulsive gamblers and panders who prey upon human weakness, children who are socially deprived and adults who are socially inadequate, rebellious adolescents and lonely pensioners, the young who at heart fear life and the old who are afraid of death, so long will there be needed men and women who are willing to pay the price of caring. In face of these incontrovertible facts let no one anticipate much less welcome, the demise of any compassionate community. There are none too many of them as it is, and, to put it mildly, The Salvation Army might be missed. For my part, I am well content to soldier on in this Christian regiment because there is no continuing city. We seek one whose builder and maker is God (Frederick Coutts, *No Continuing City*).

A New Year Bride

We helped to save her from the life
To which her father sold her.
And today,
This New Year's Day,
She is a bride.

A lovely bit of cloth,
All plum-strewn,
Was her parting gift to me . . .
I cannot gaze upon those flowers enough!

Tamiko Yamamuro (translated from the Japanese by Lois J. Erickson)